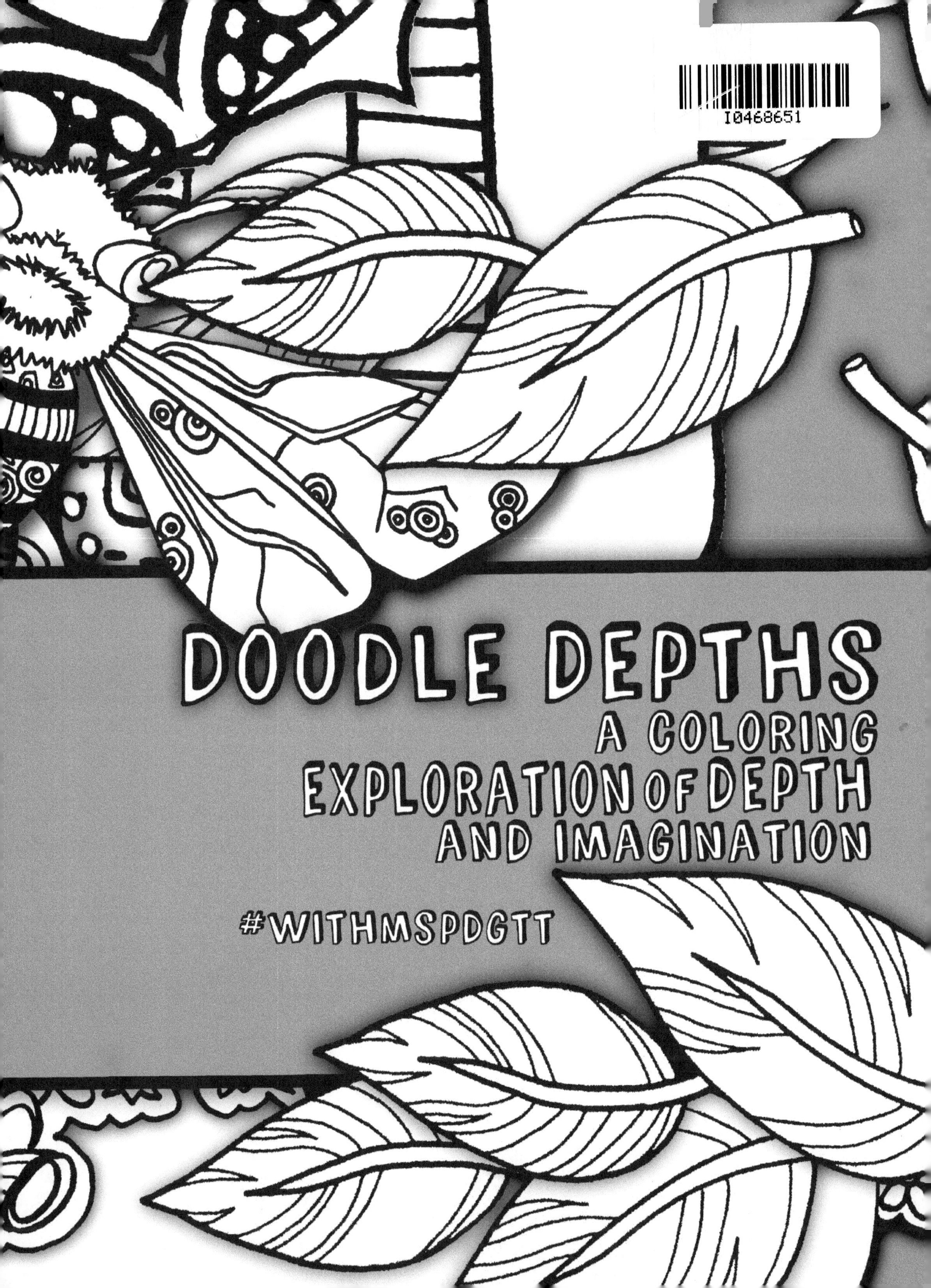
DOODLE DEPTHS
A COLORING
EXPLORATION OF DEPTH
AND IMAGINATION
#WITHMSPDGTT

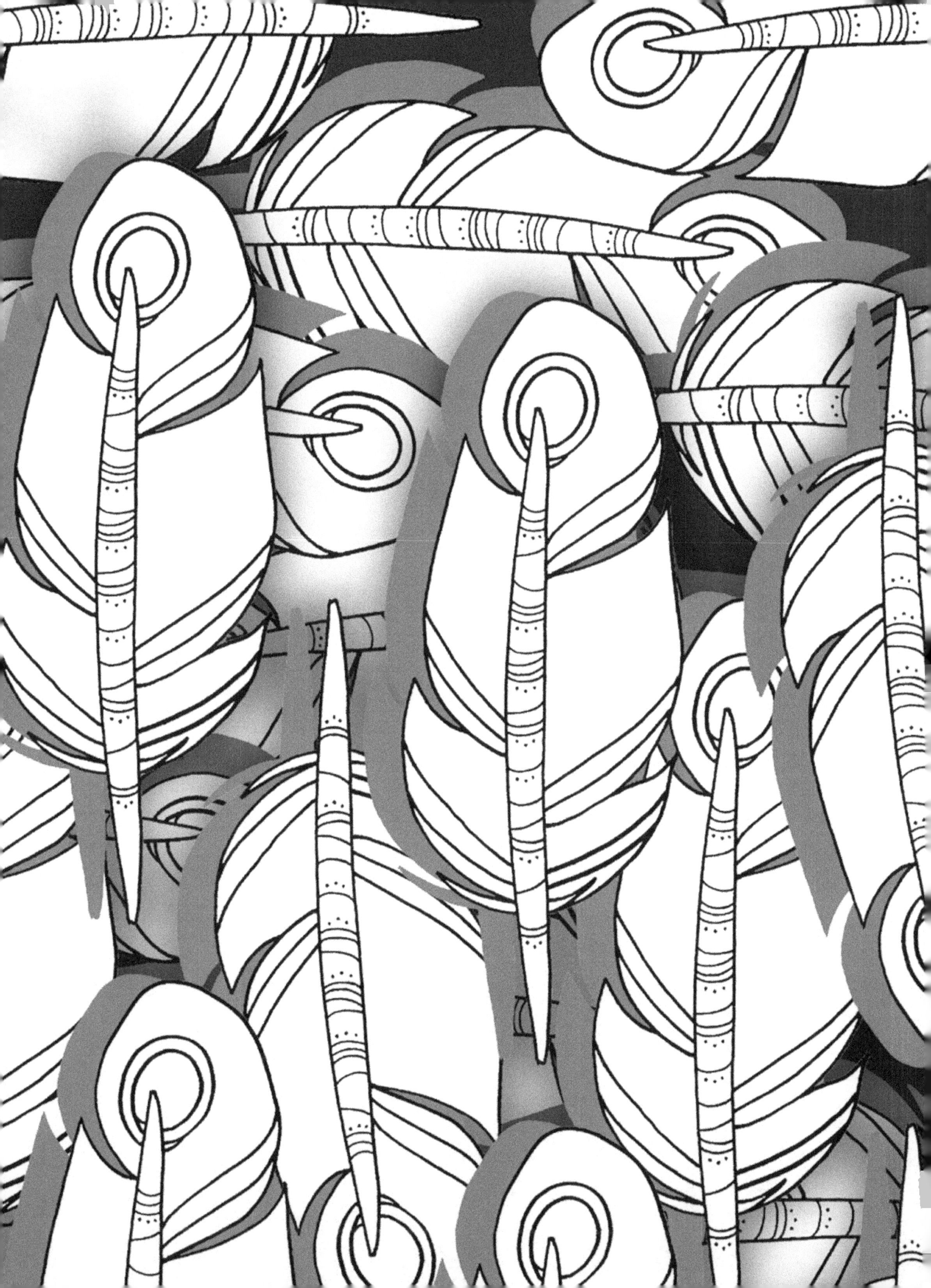

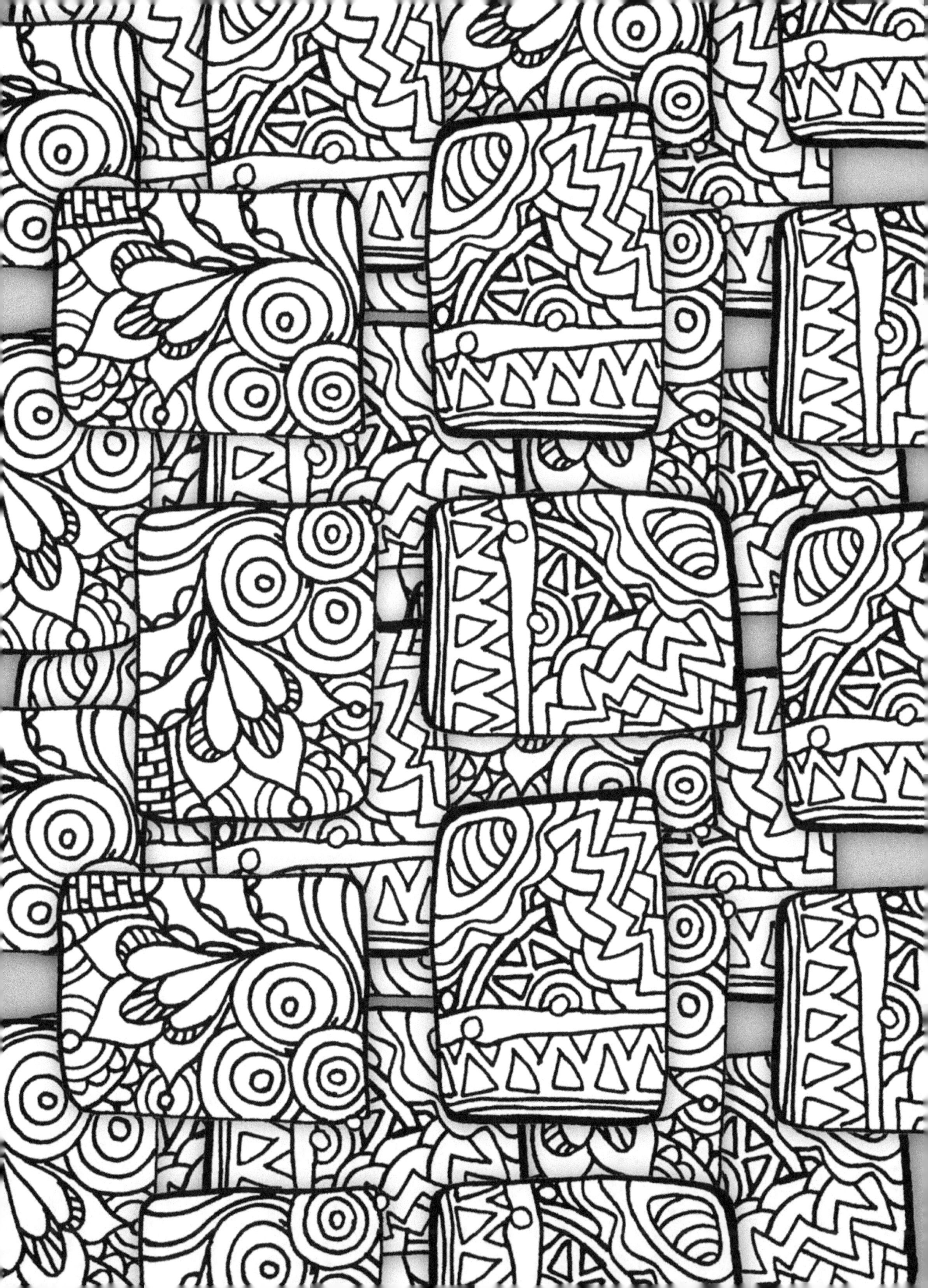

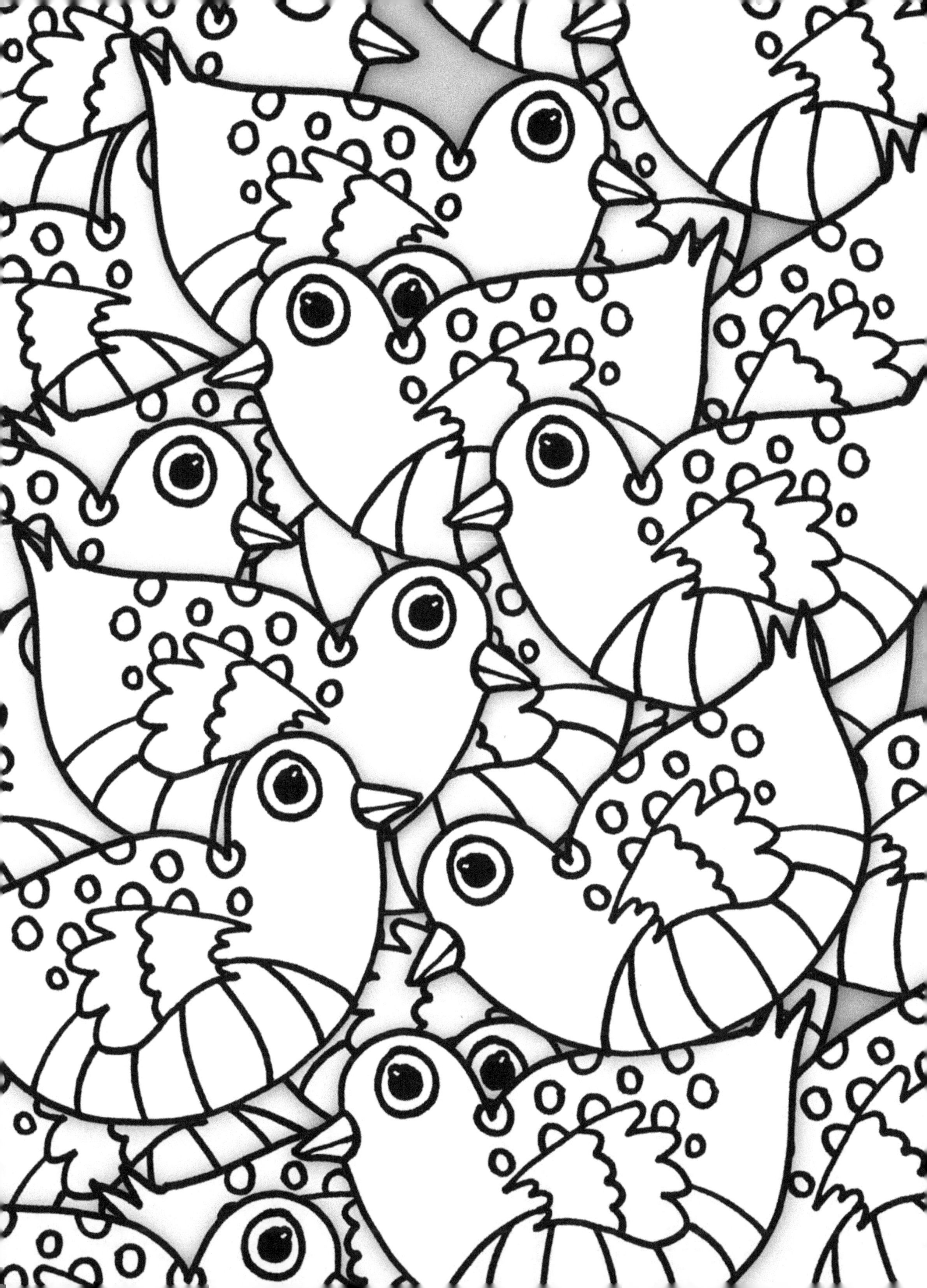

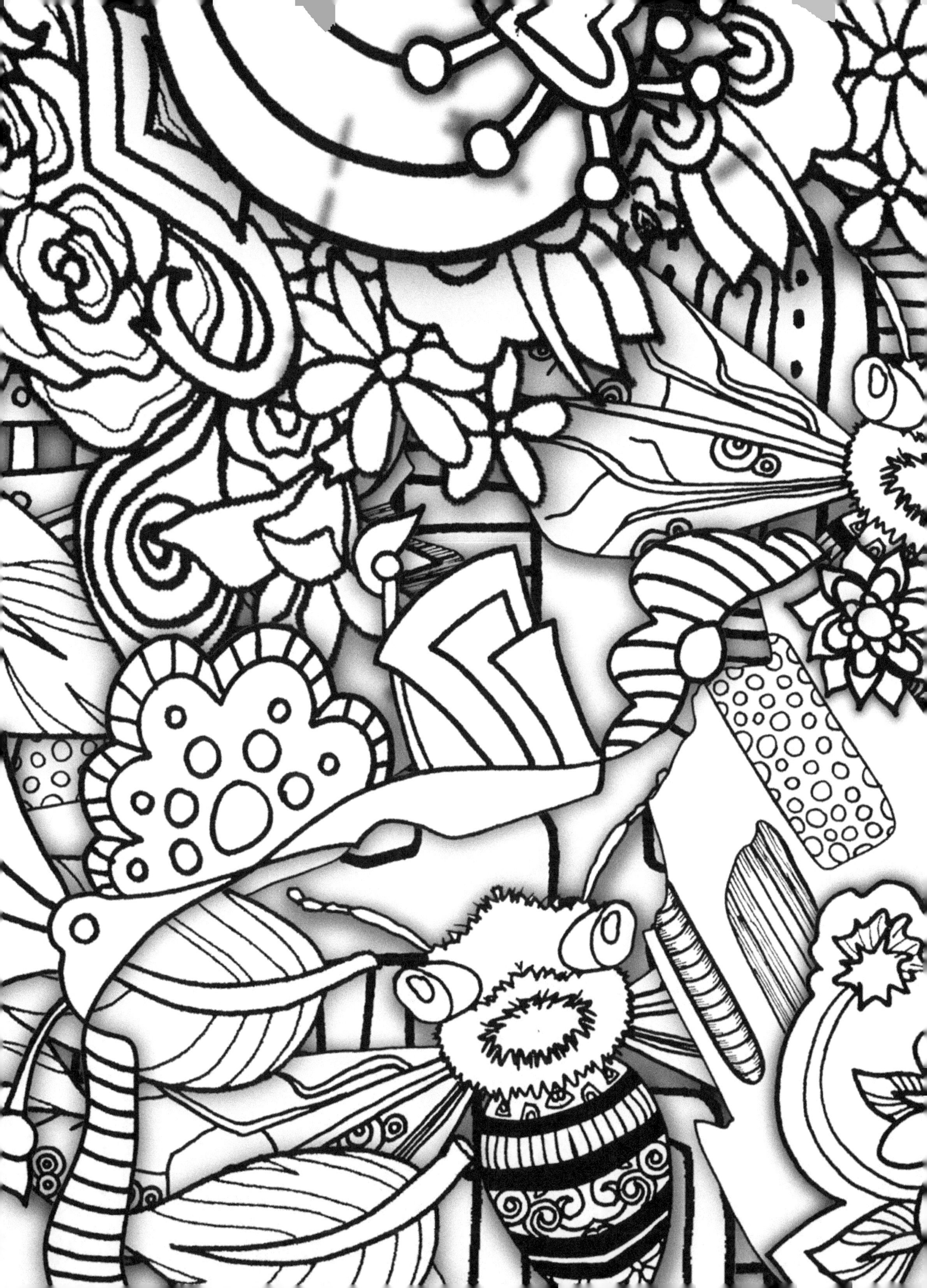

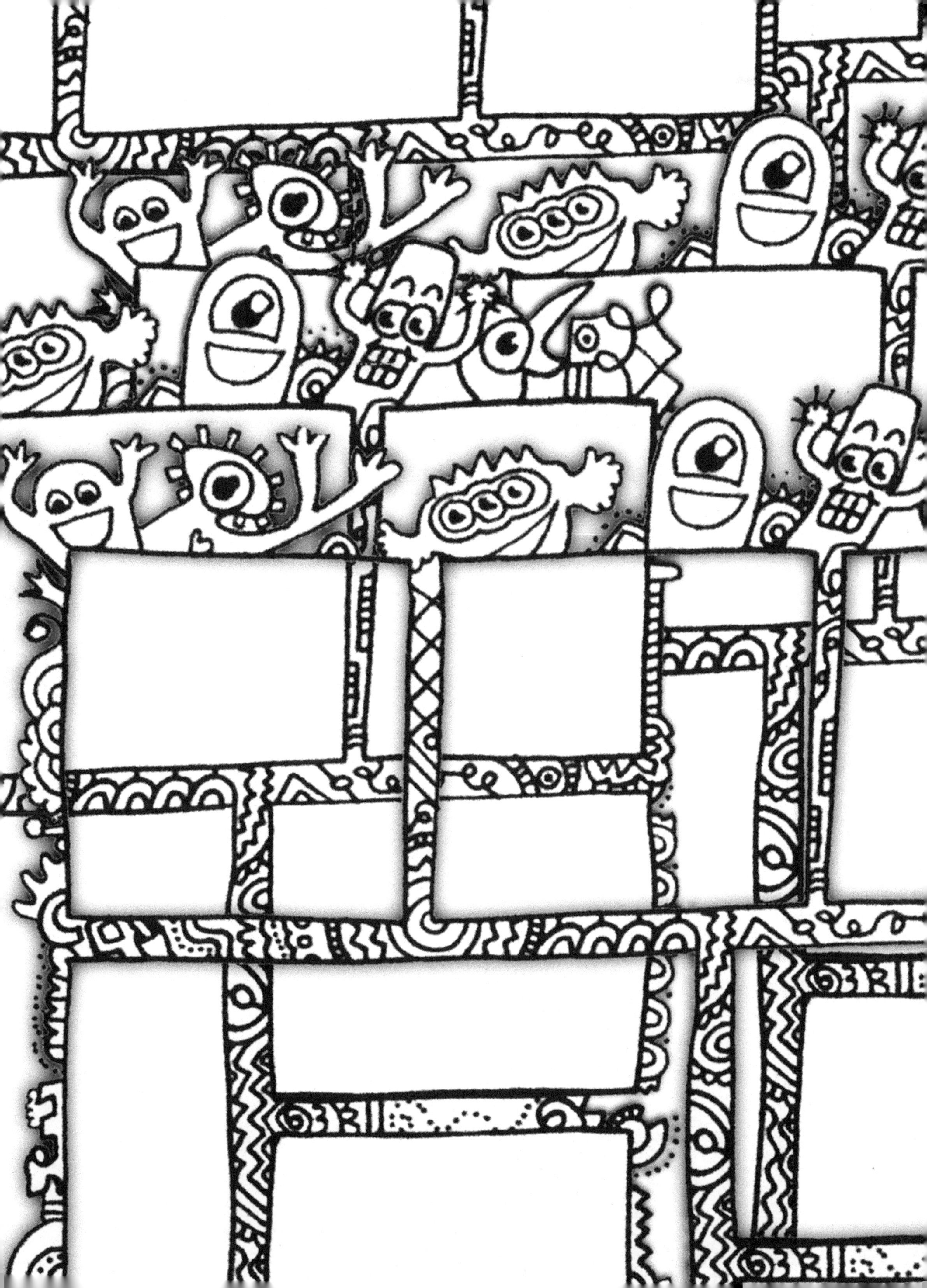

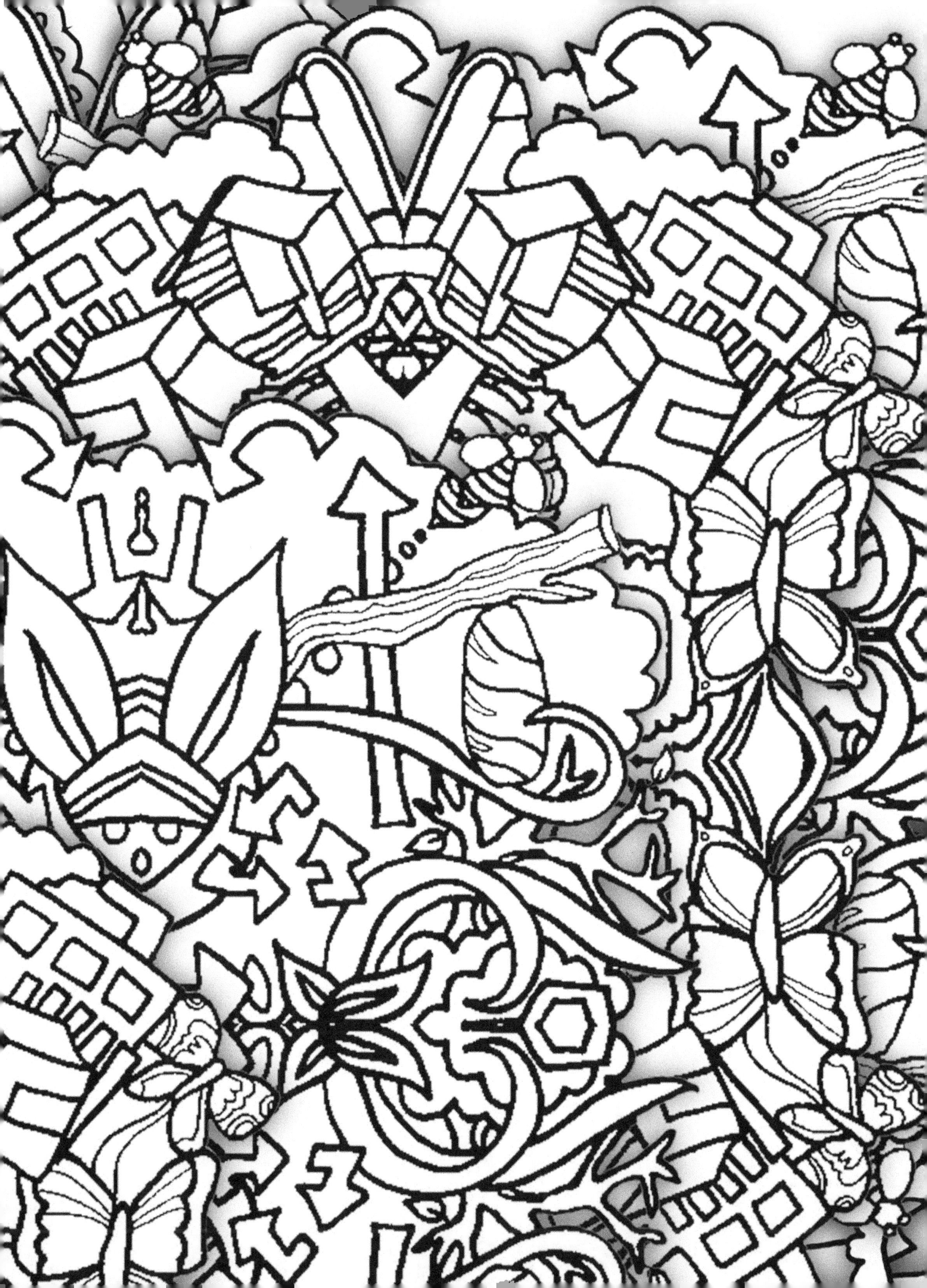

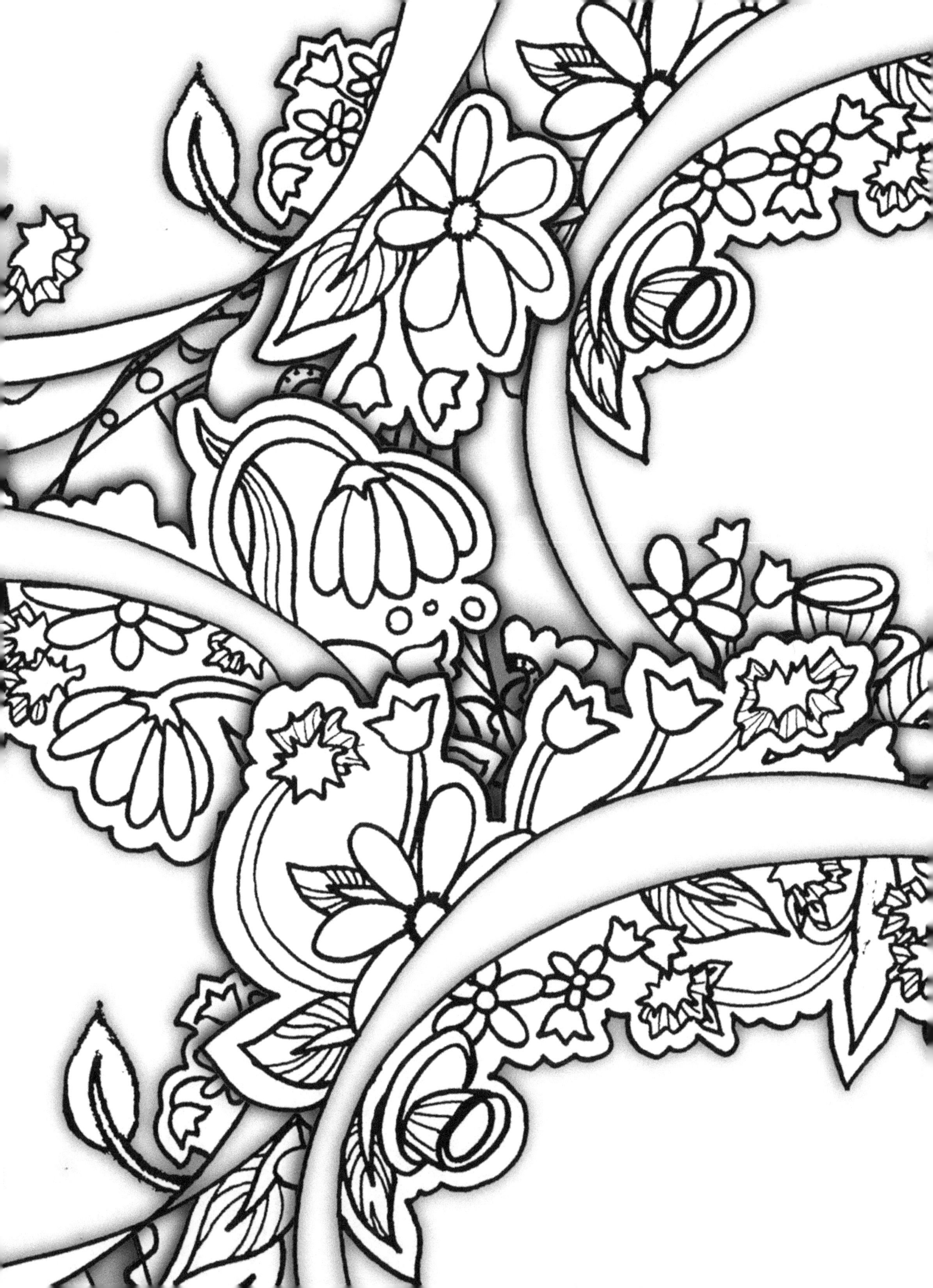

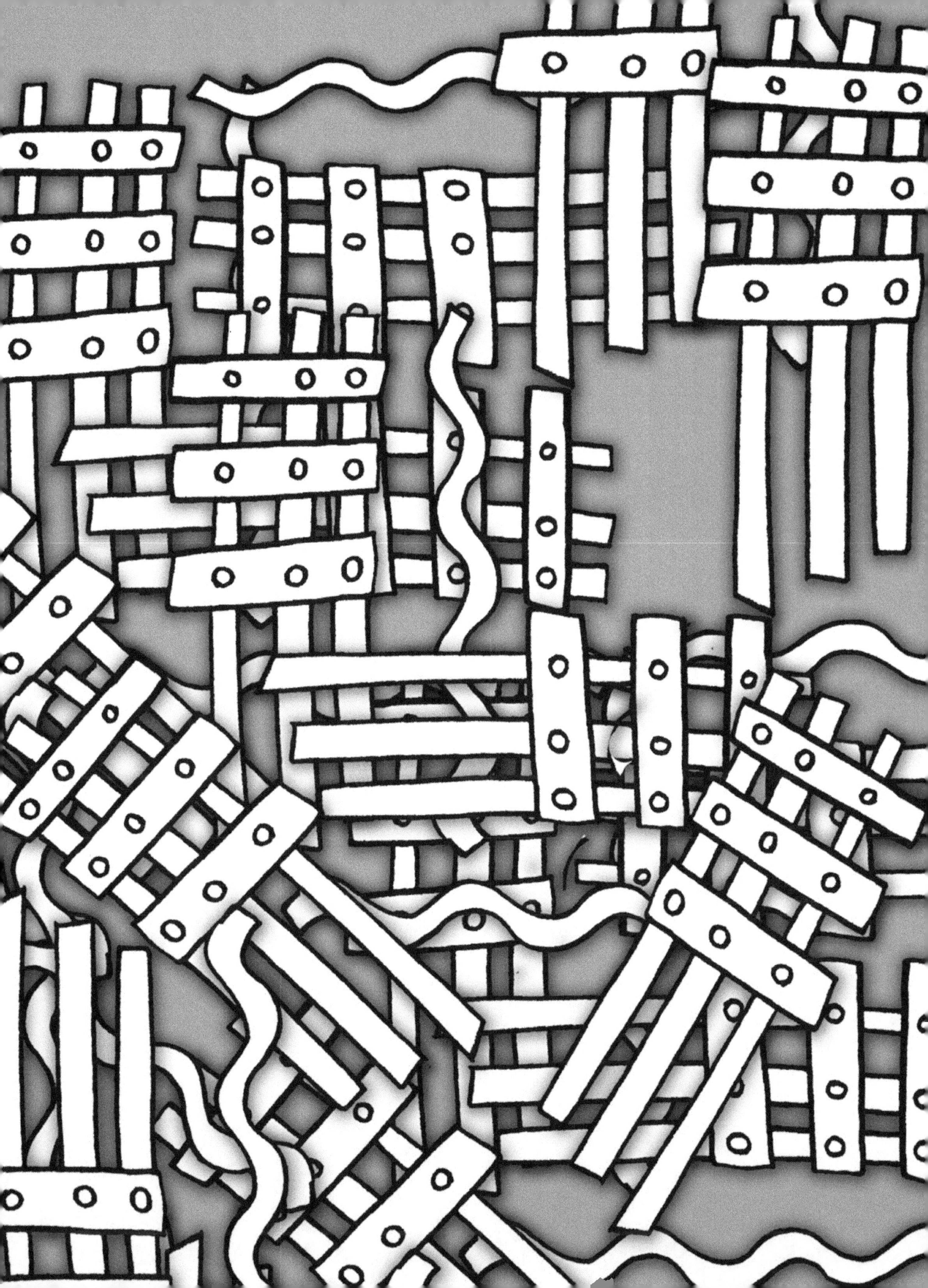

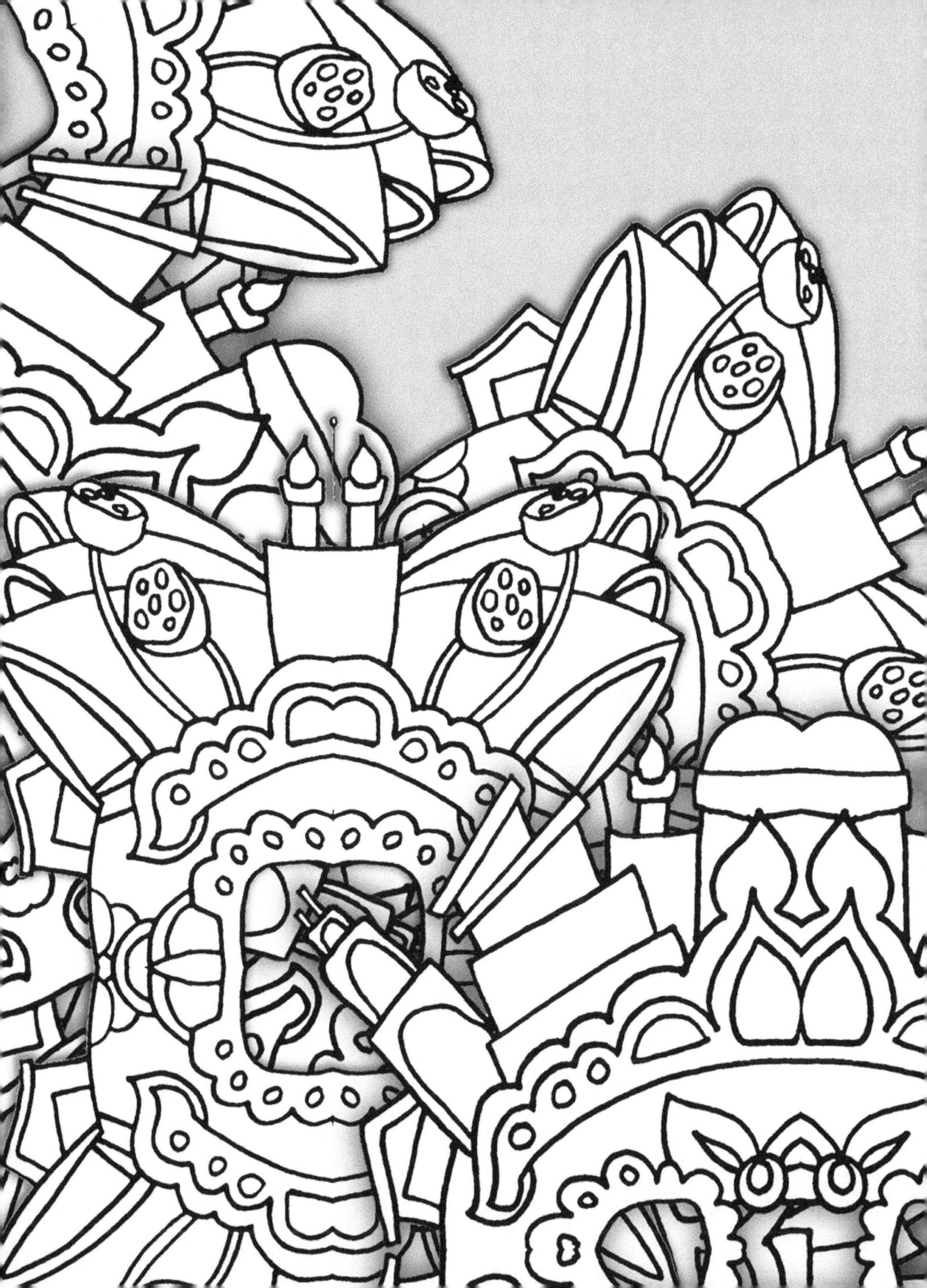

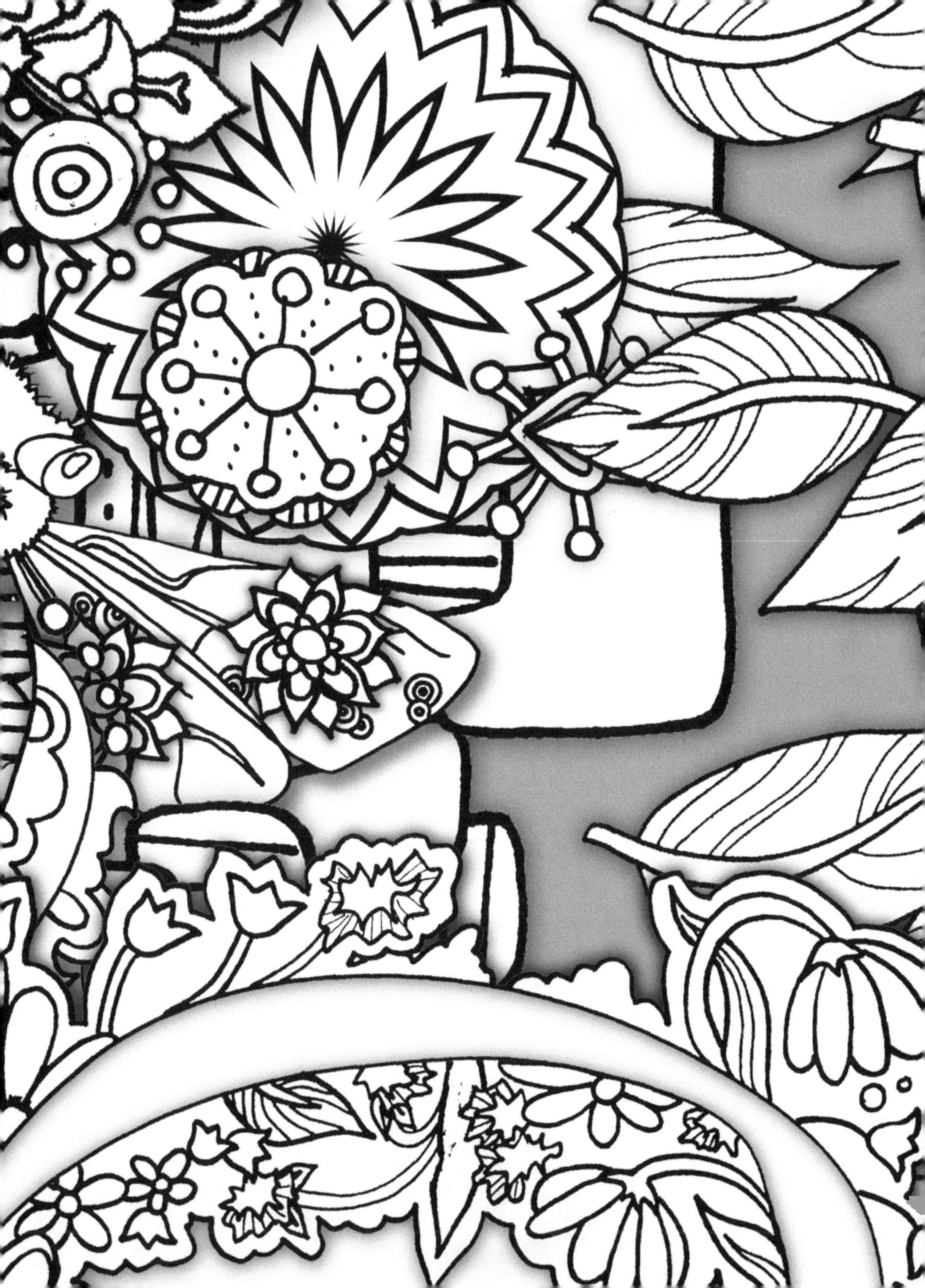

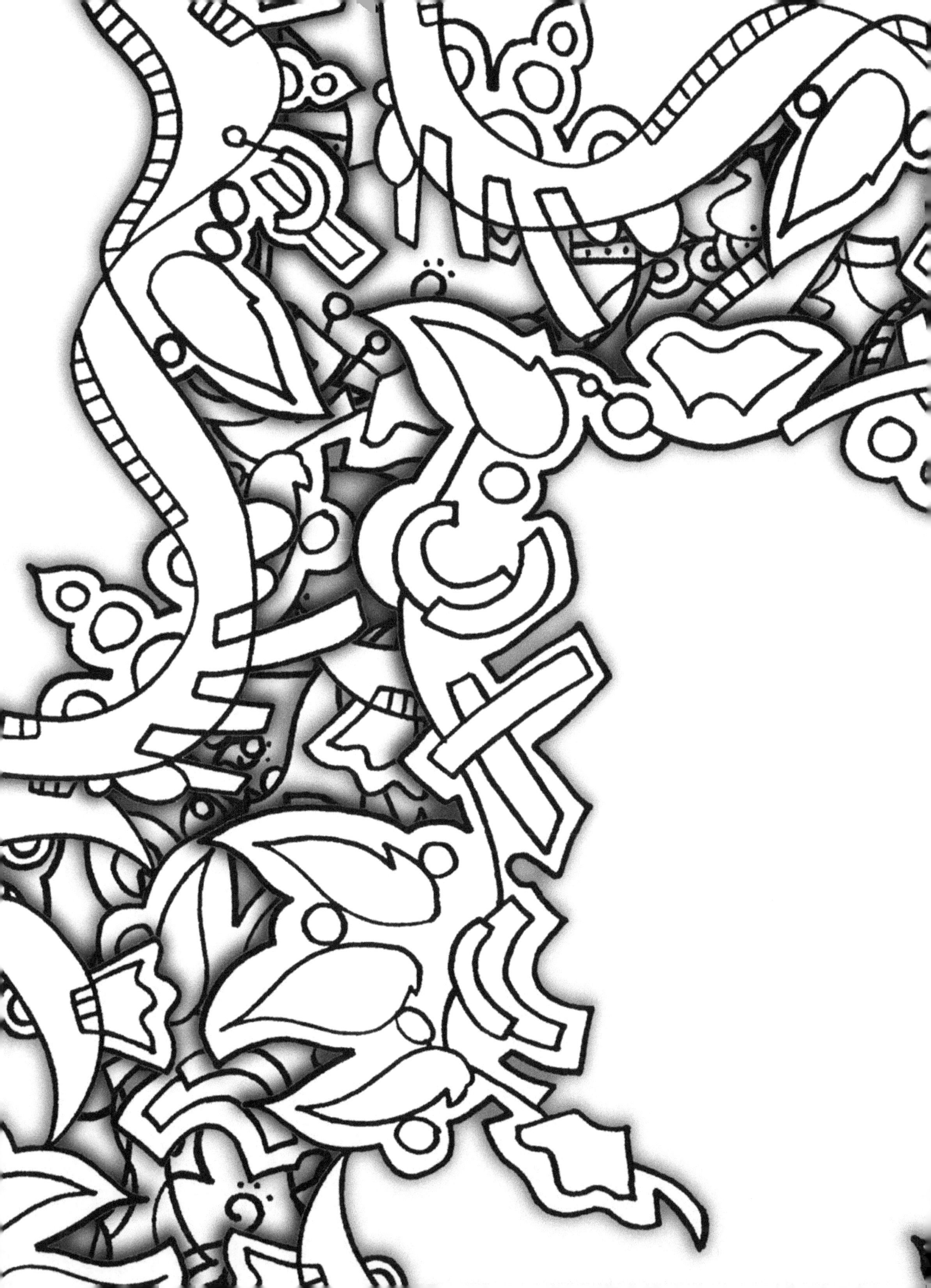

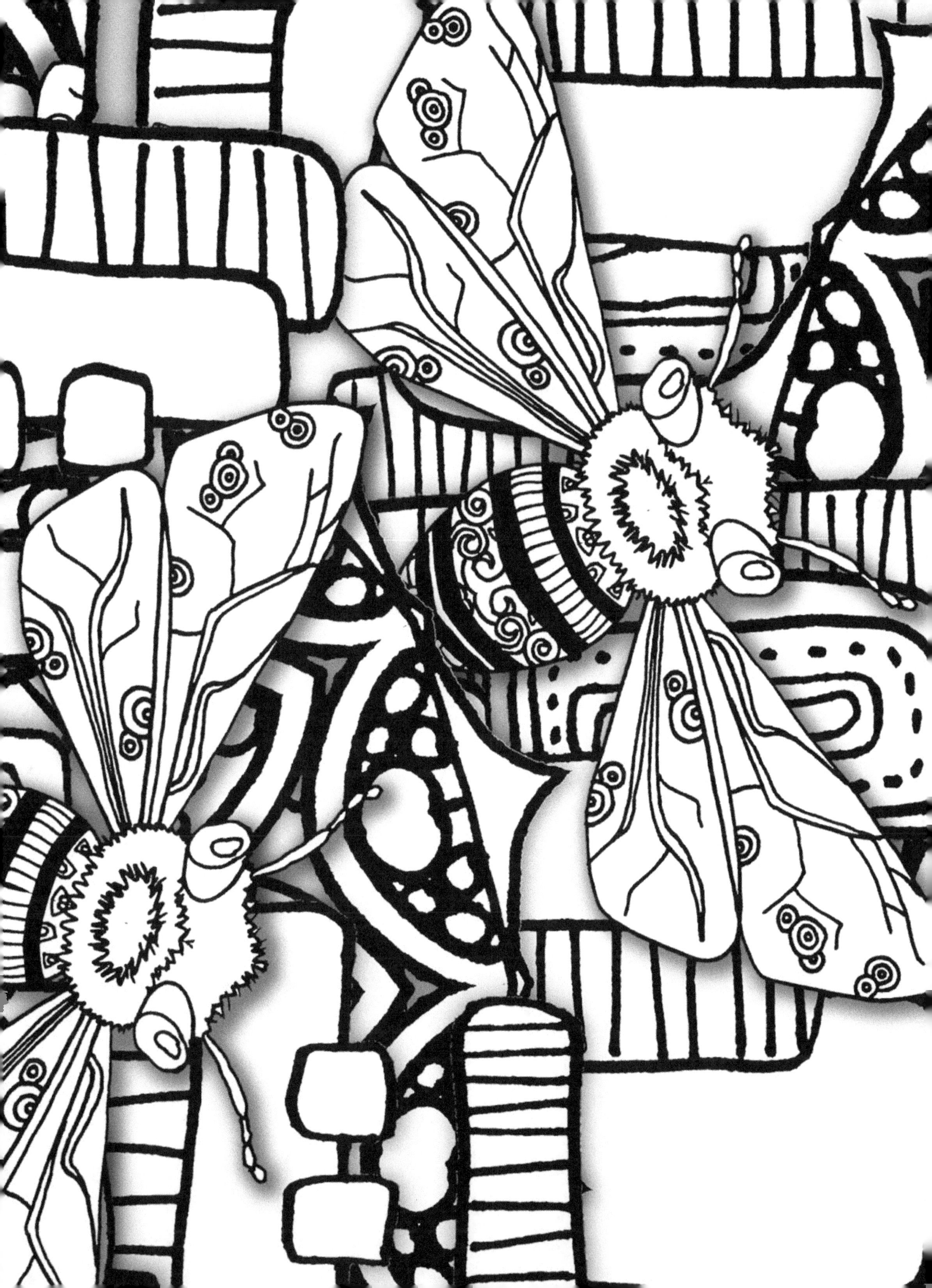

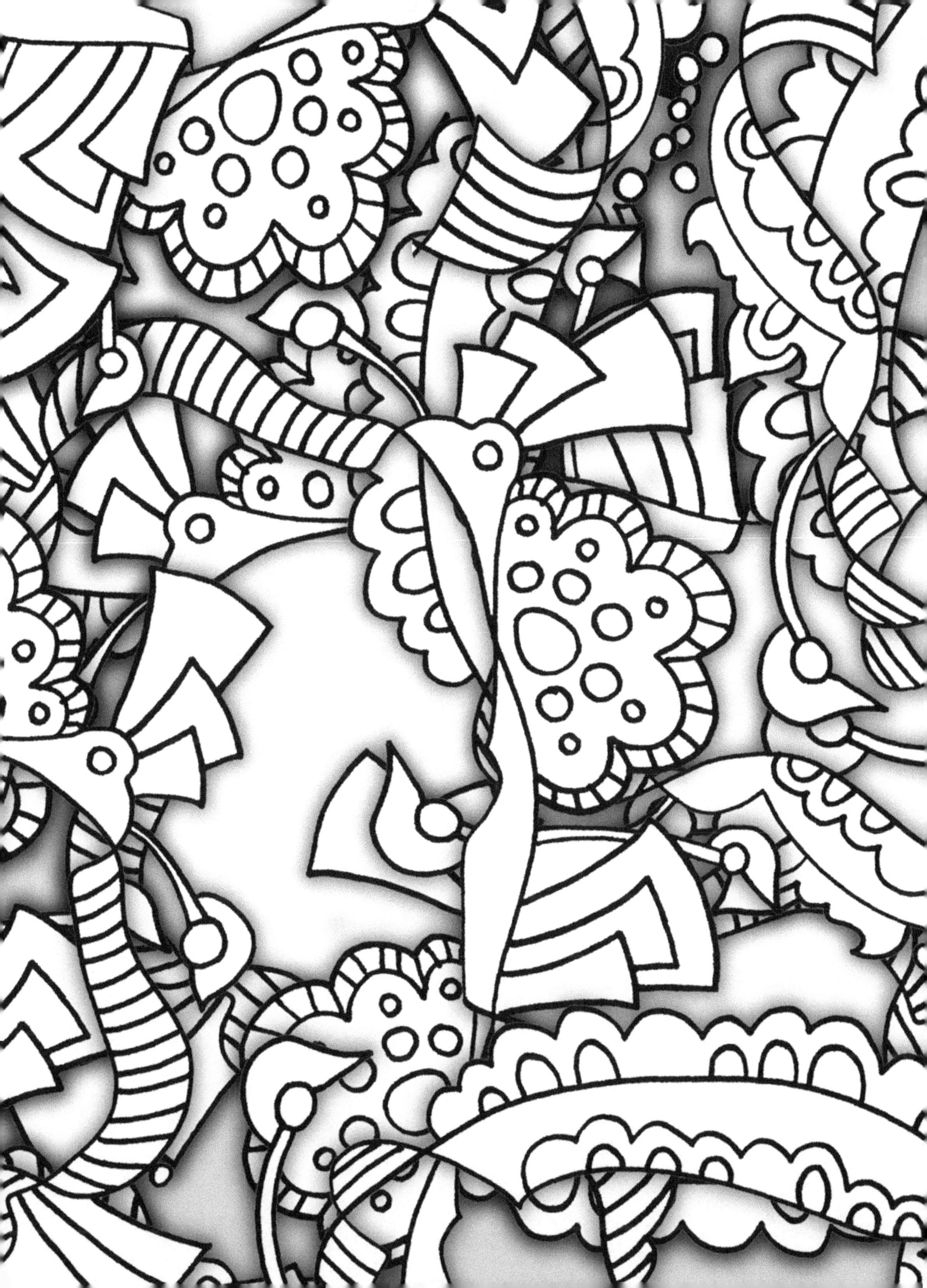

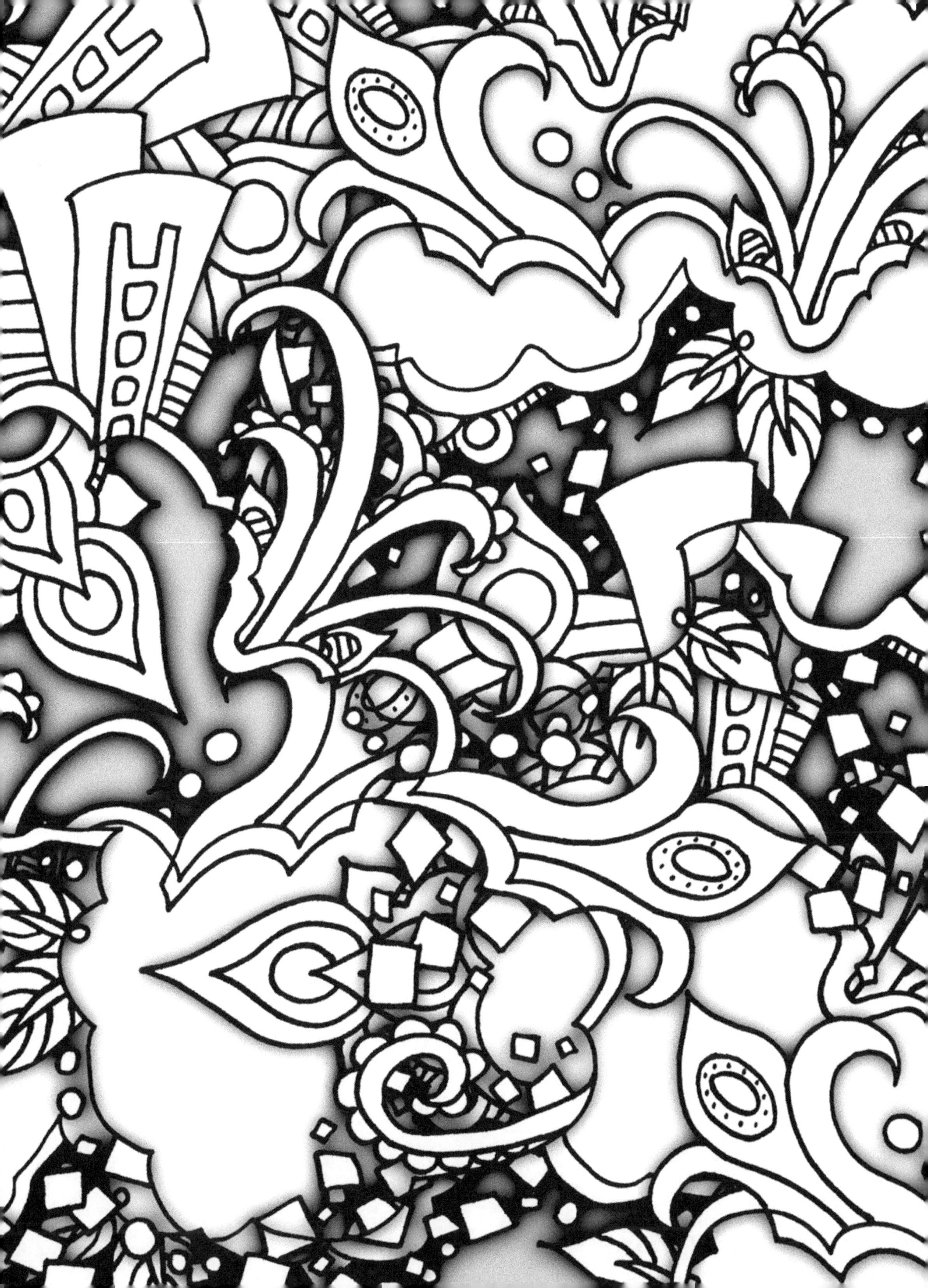

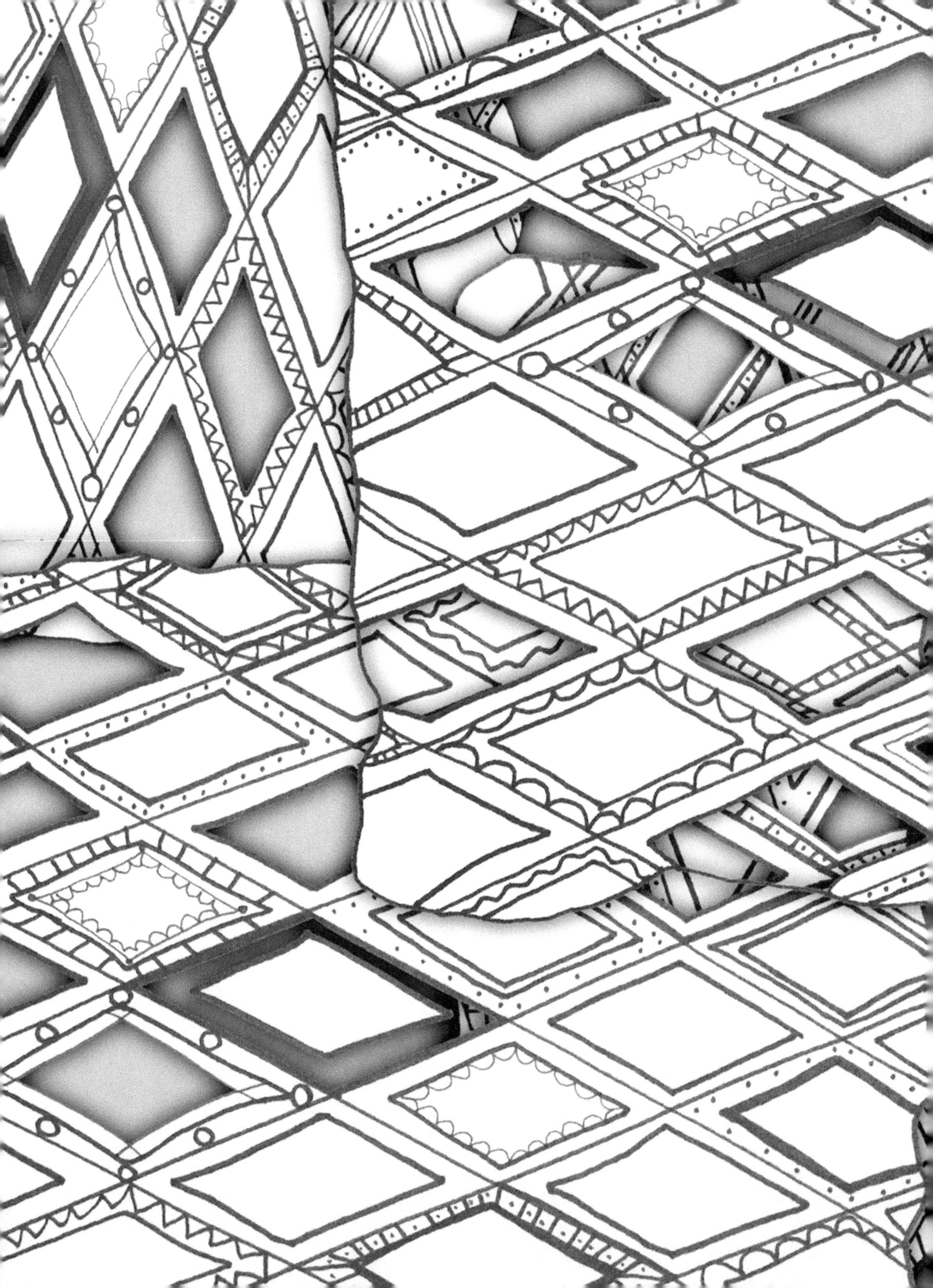

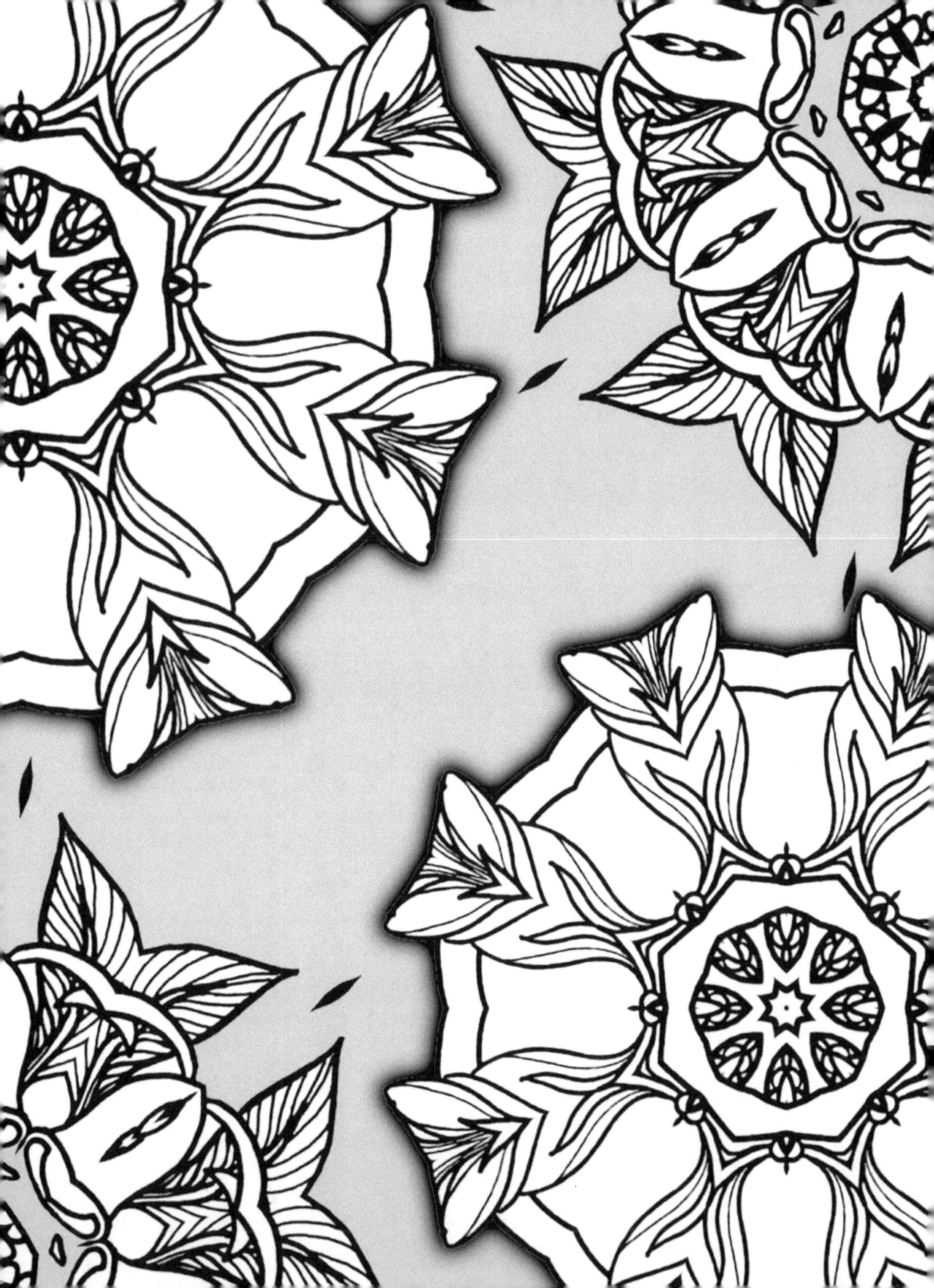

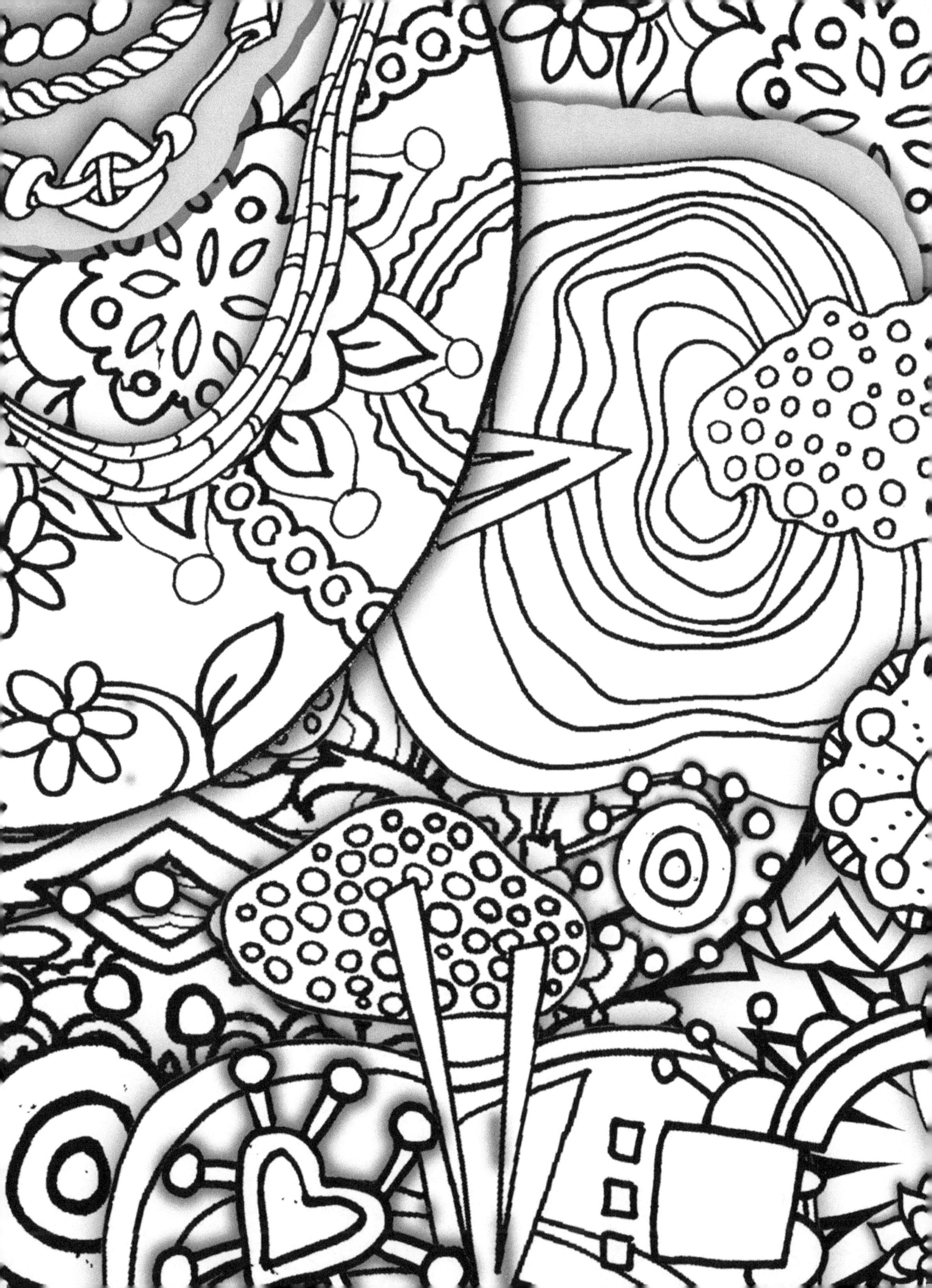

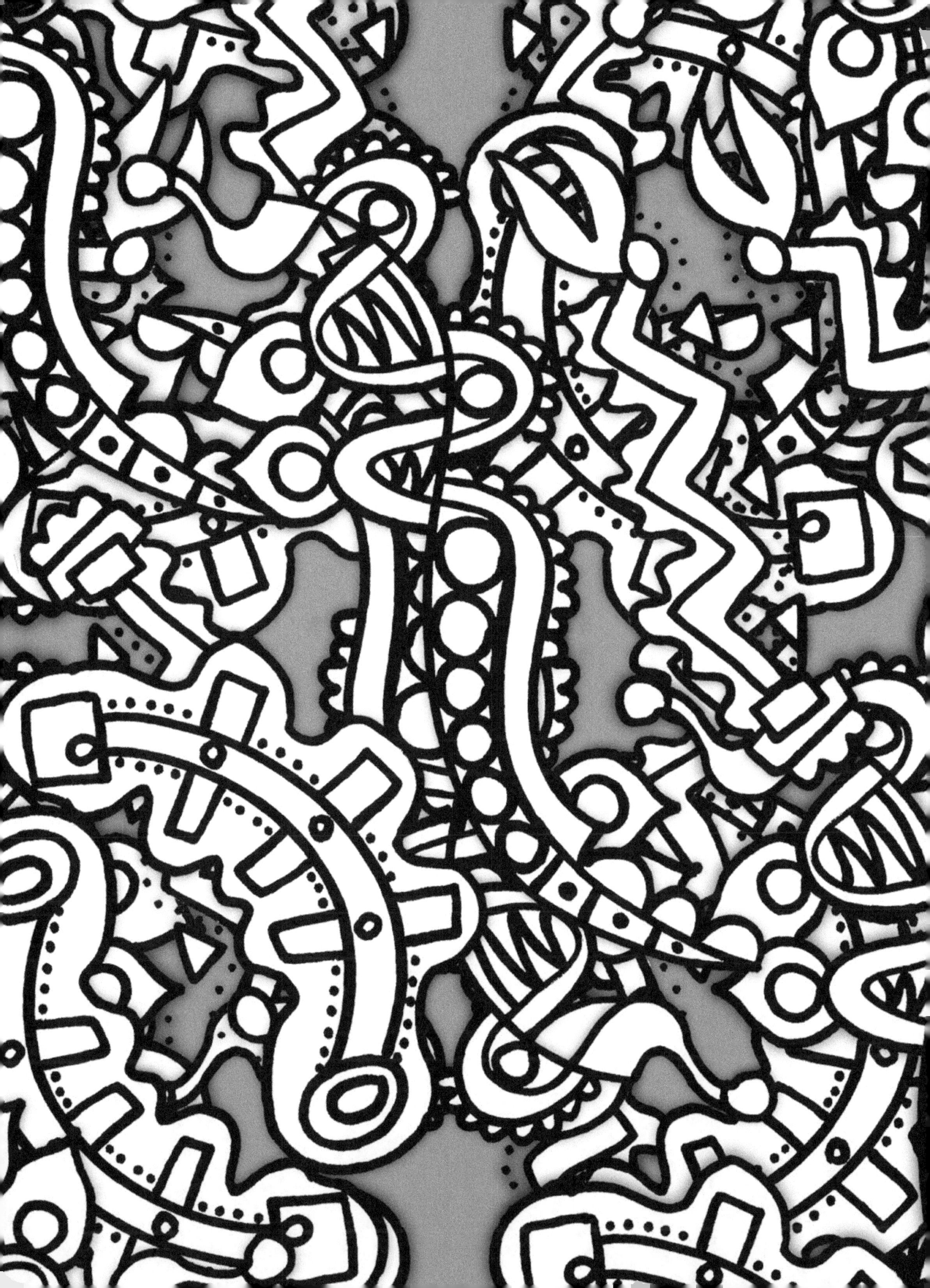

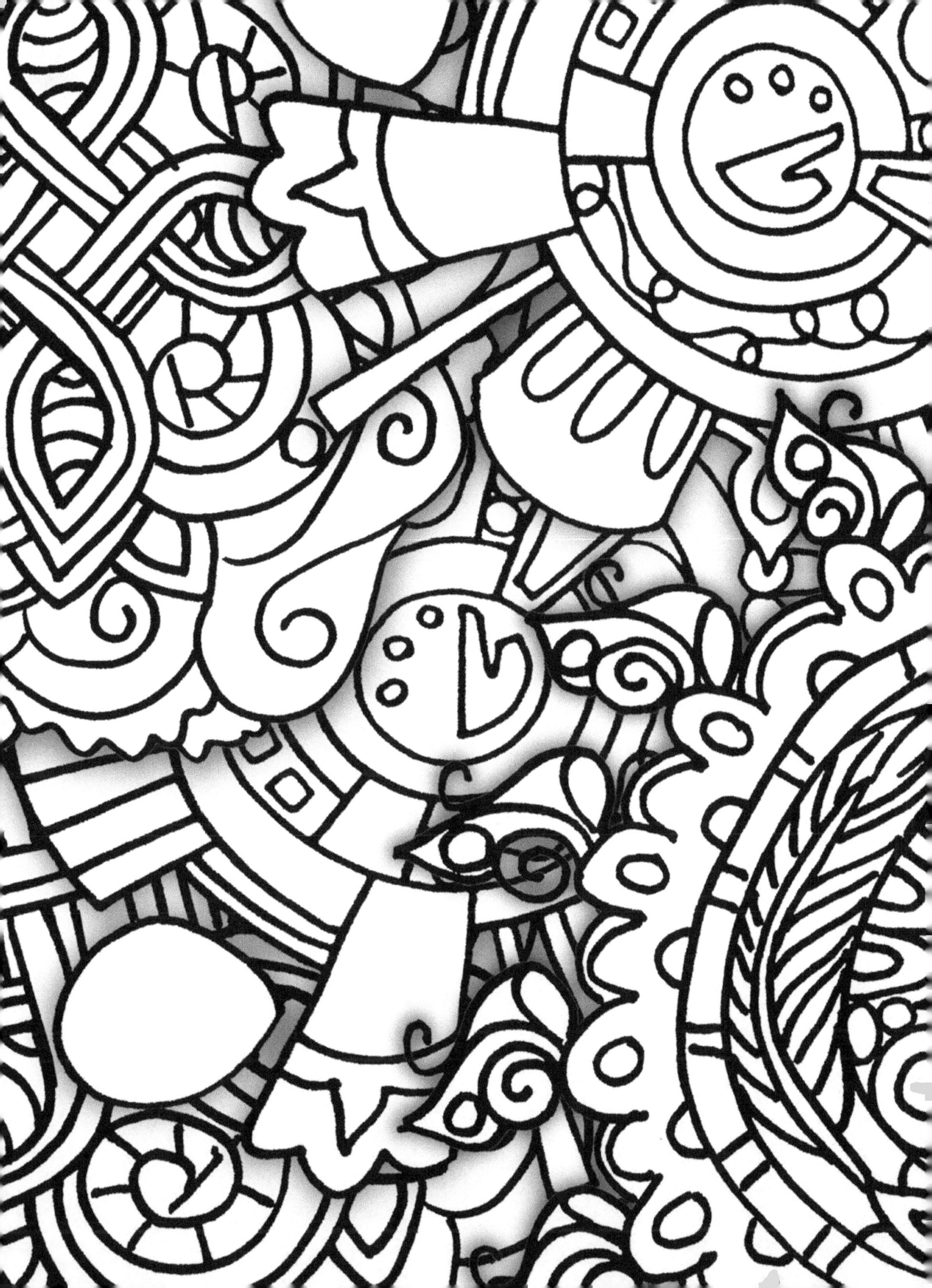

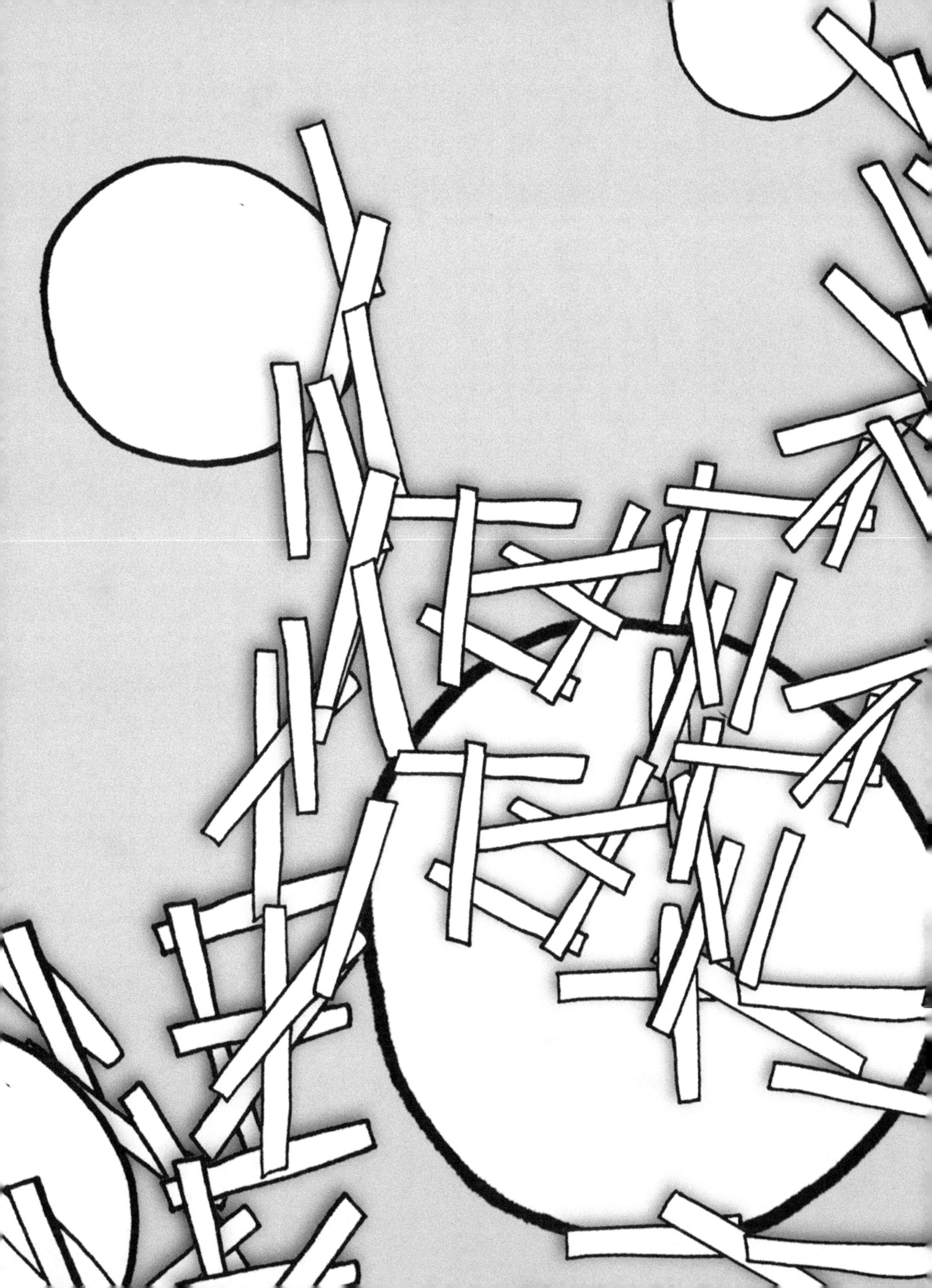

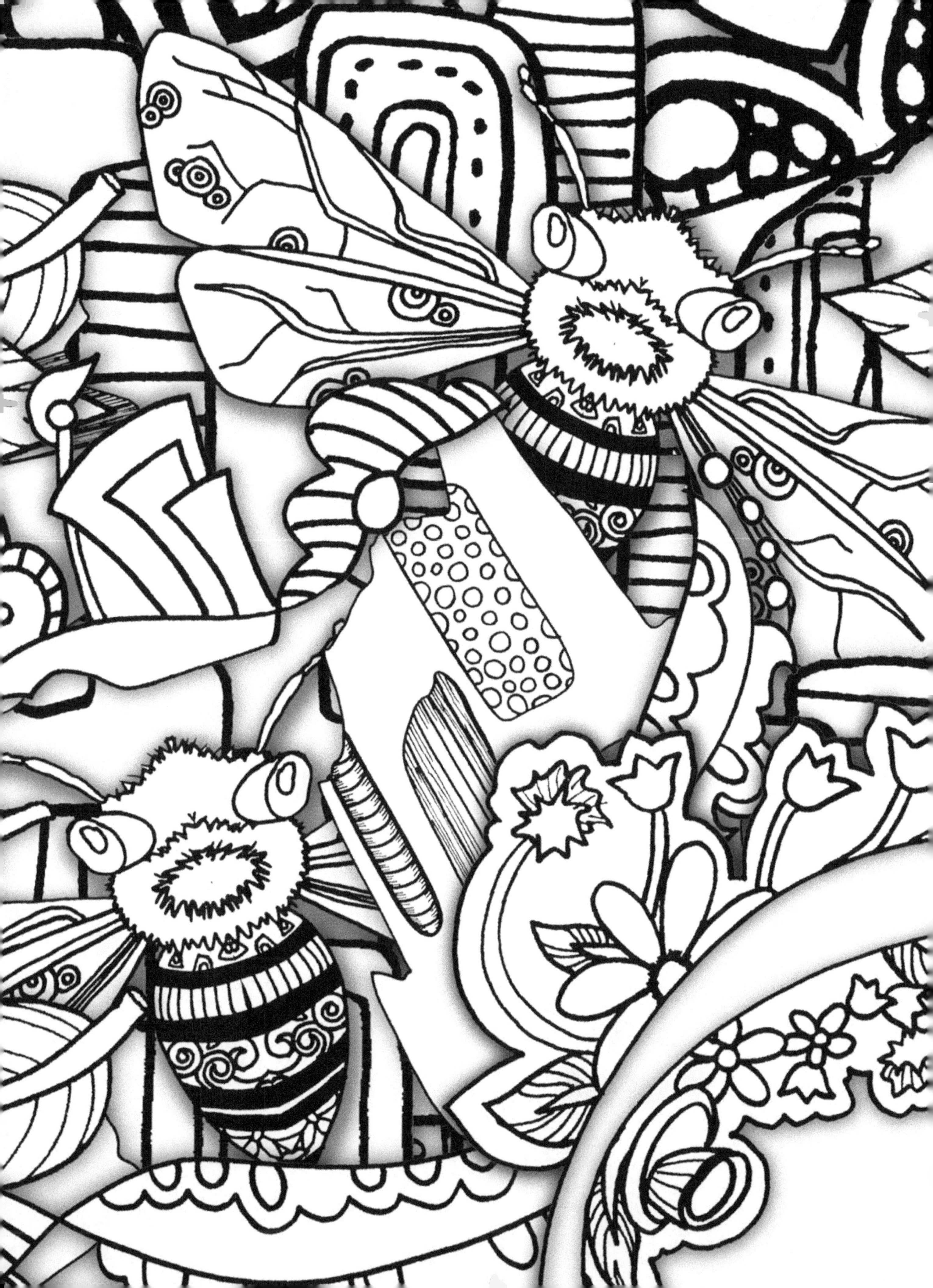

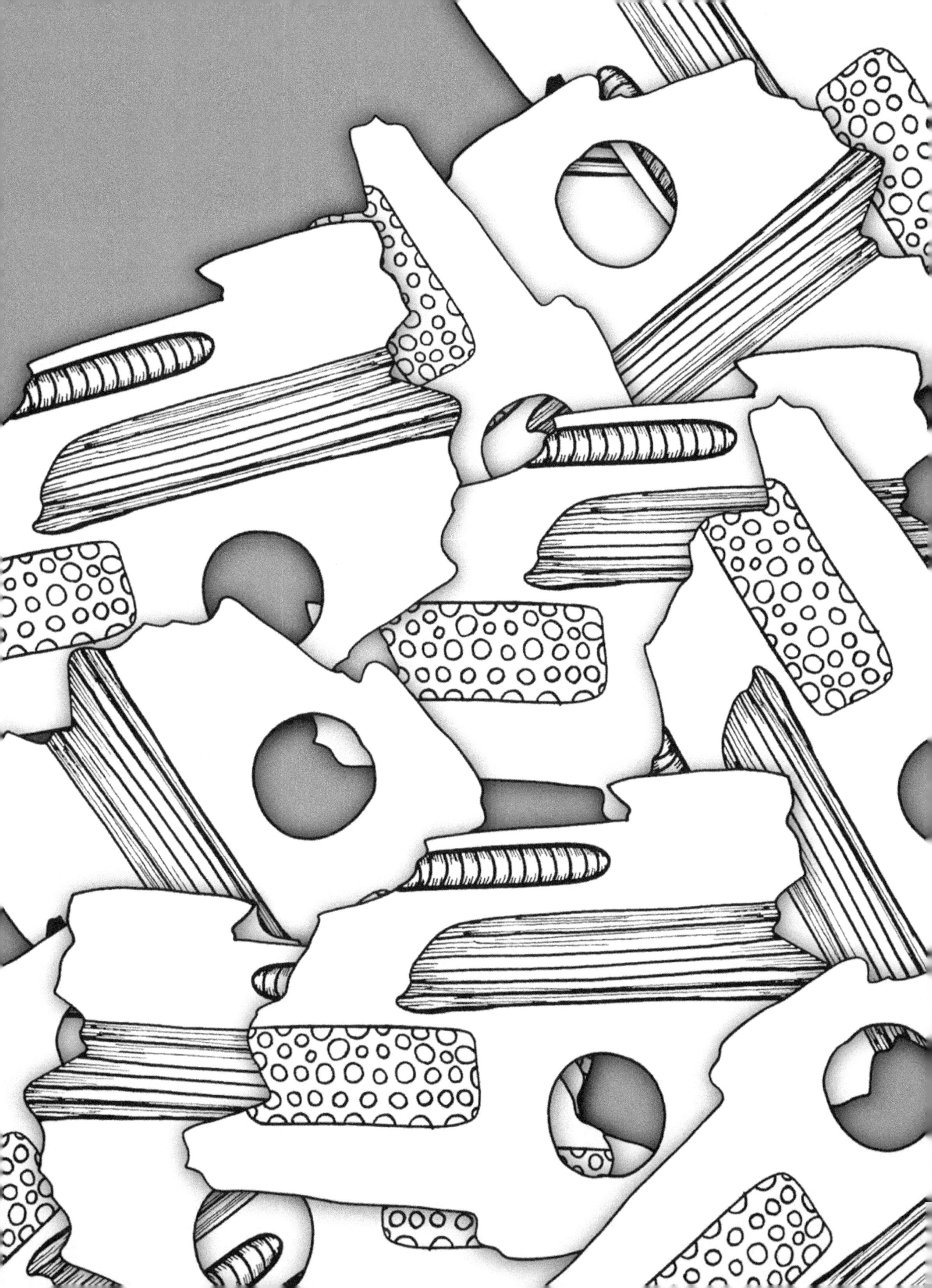

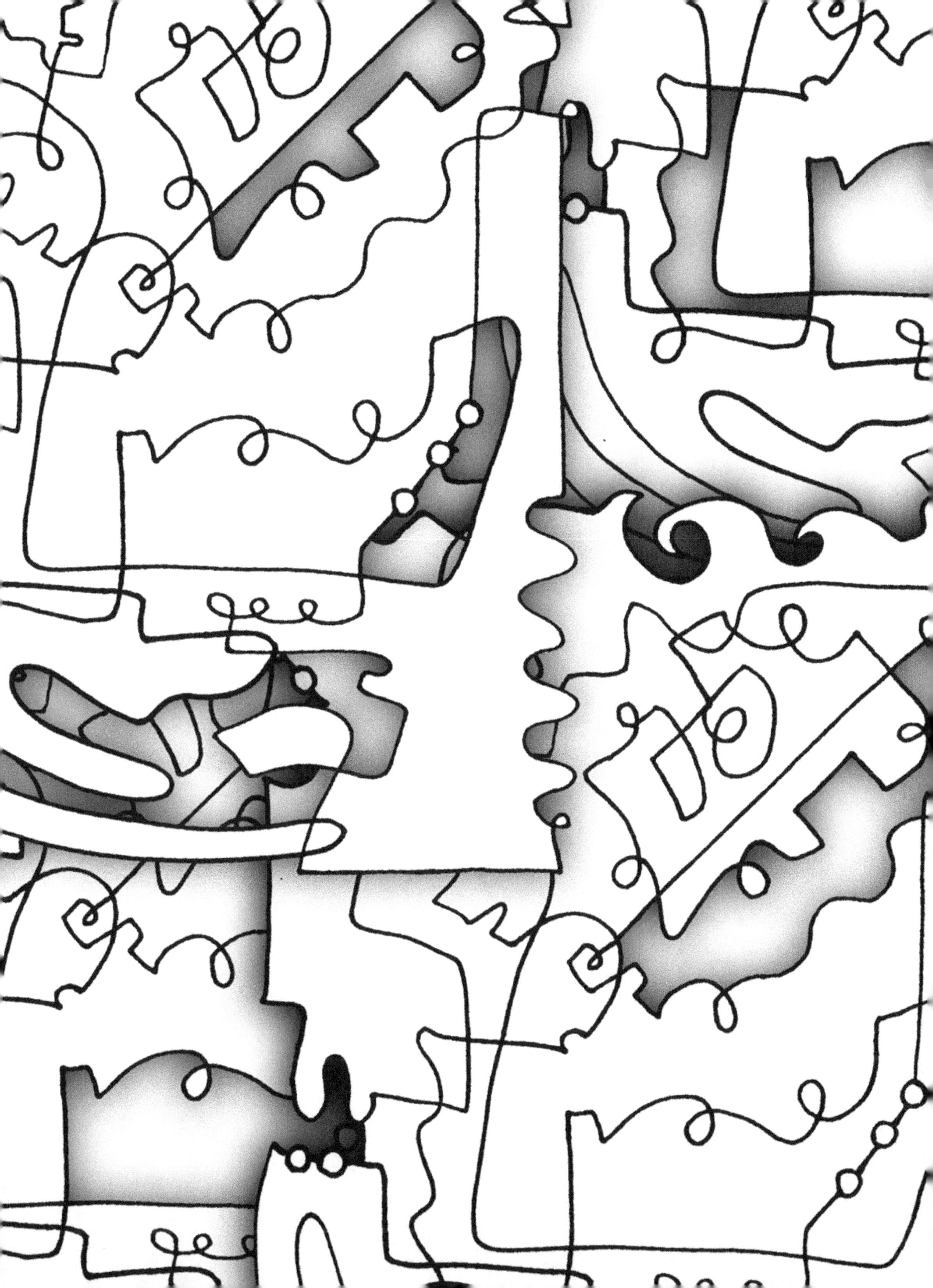

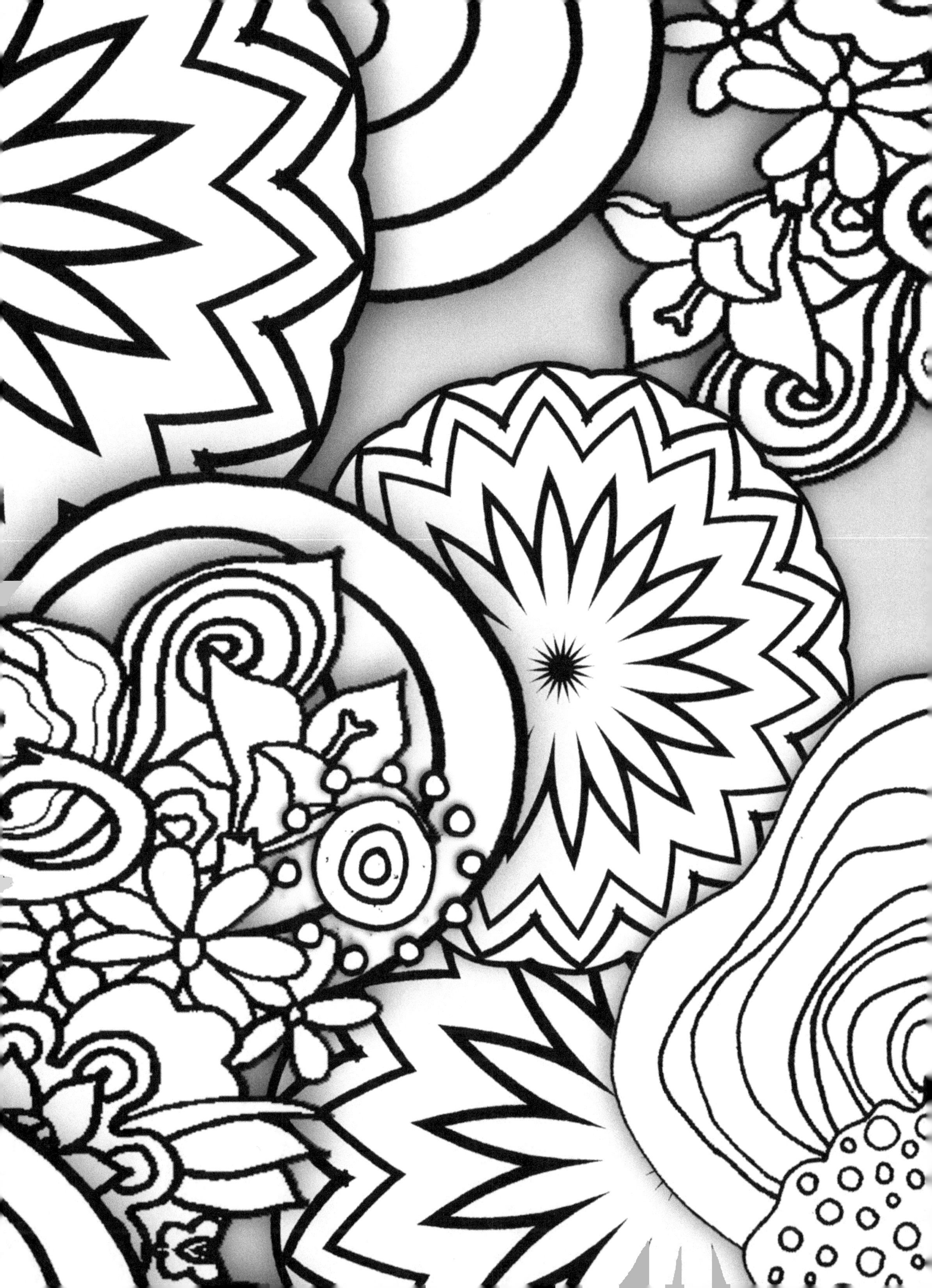

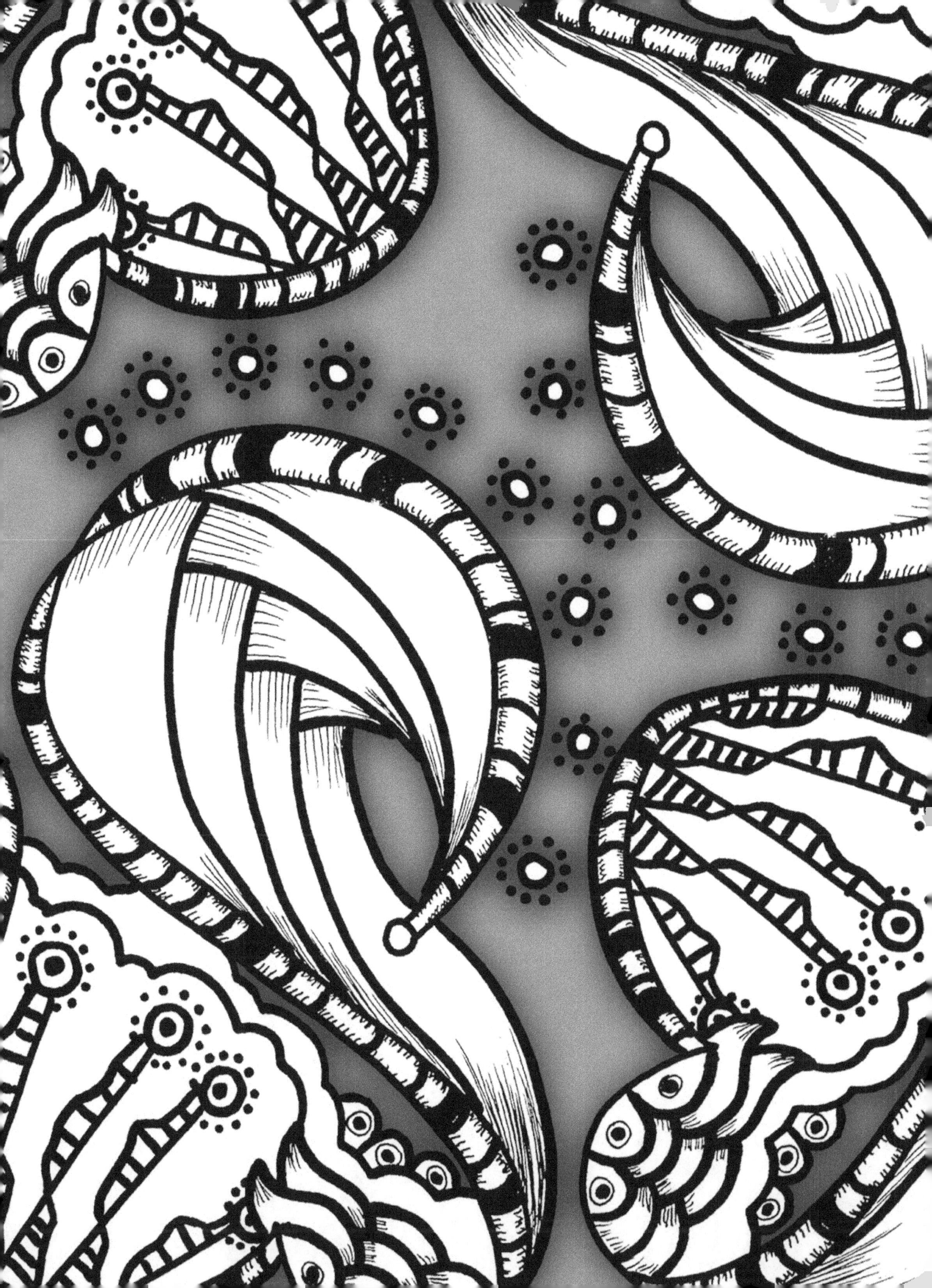

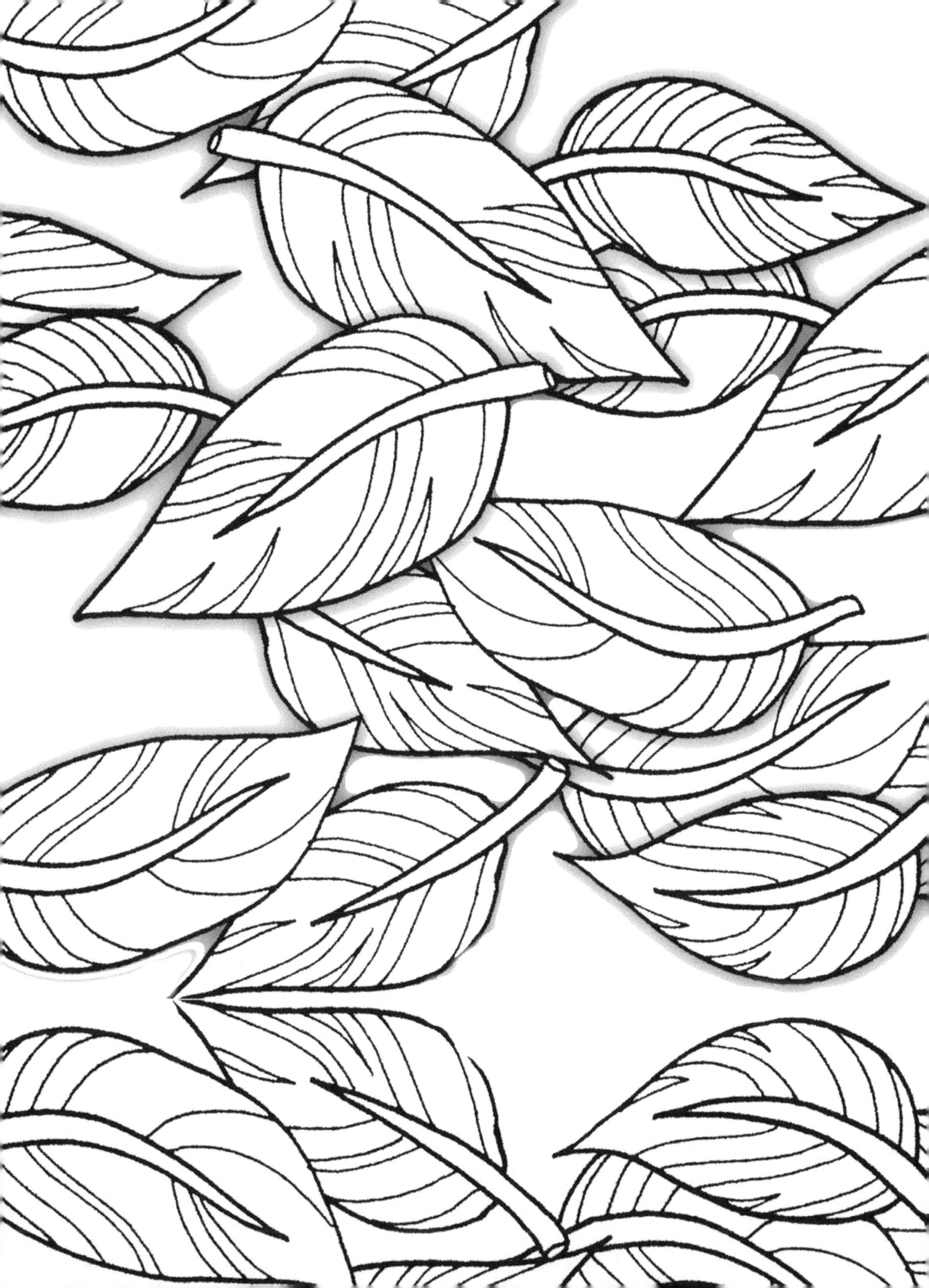

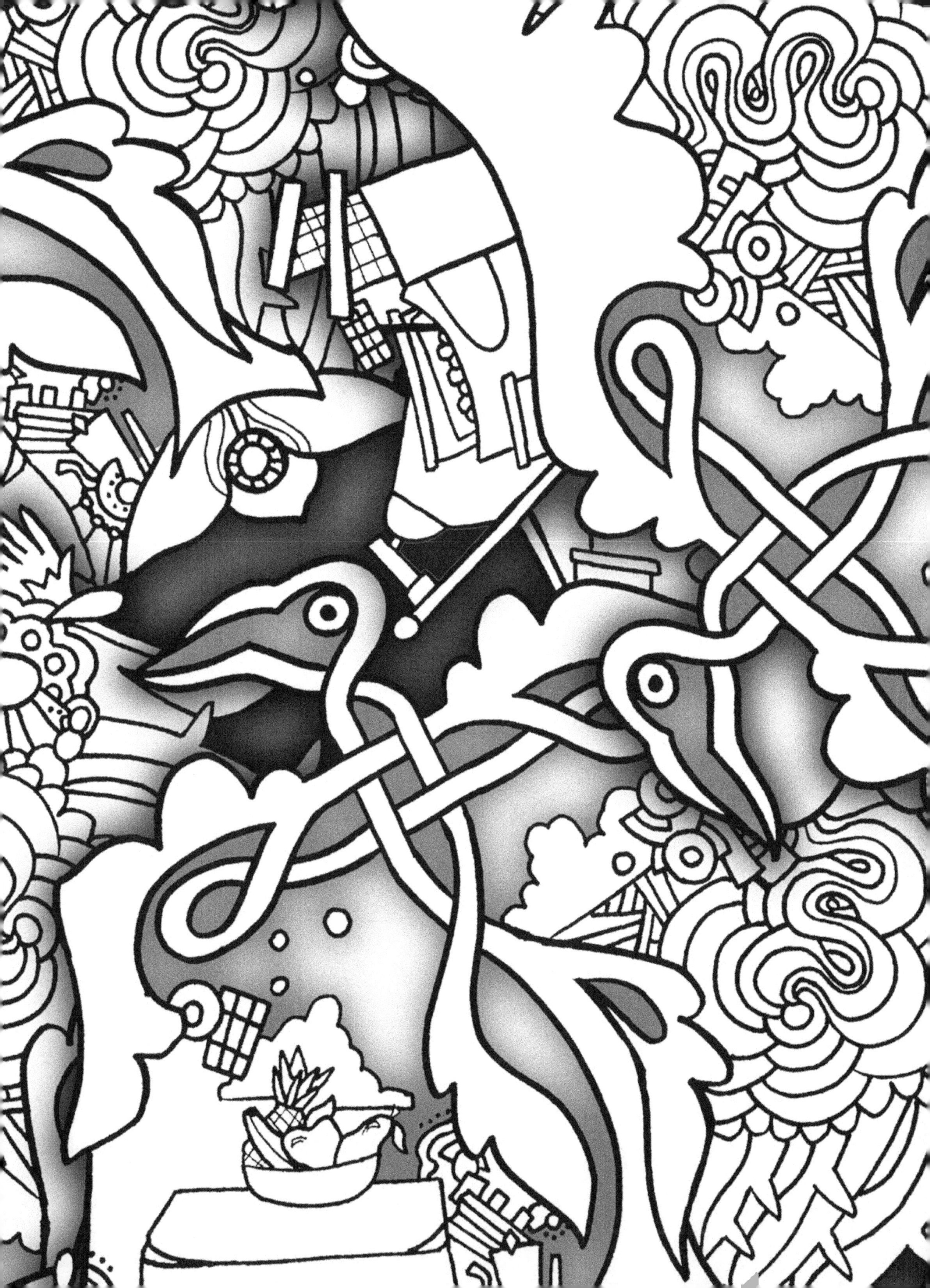

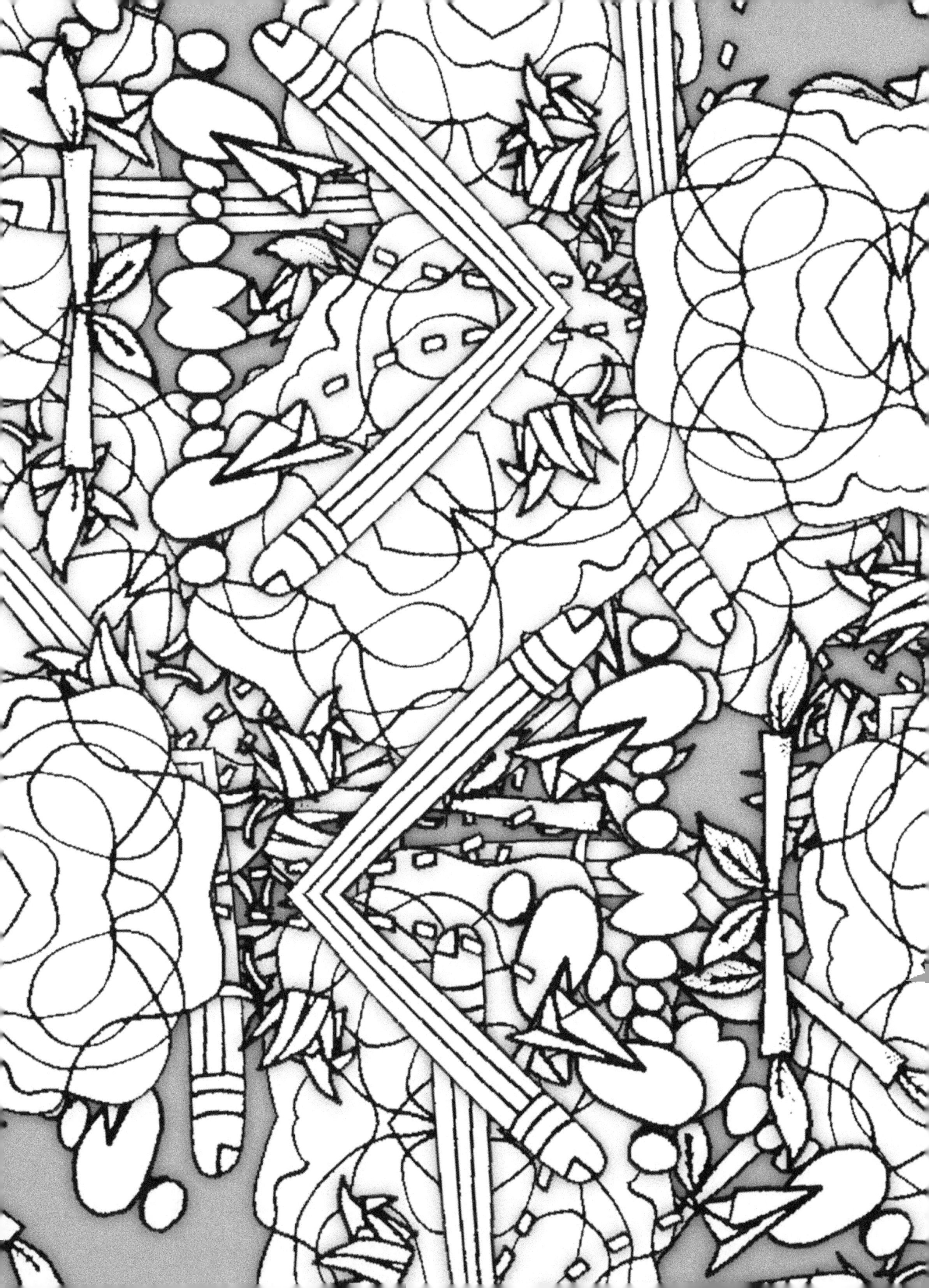

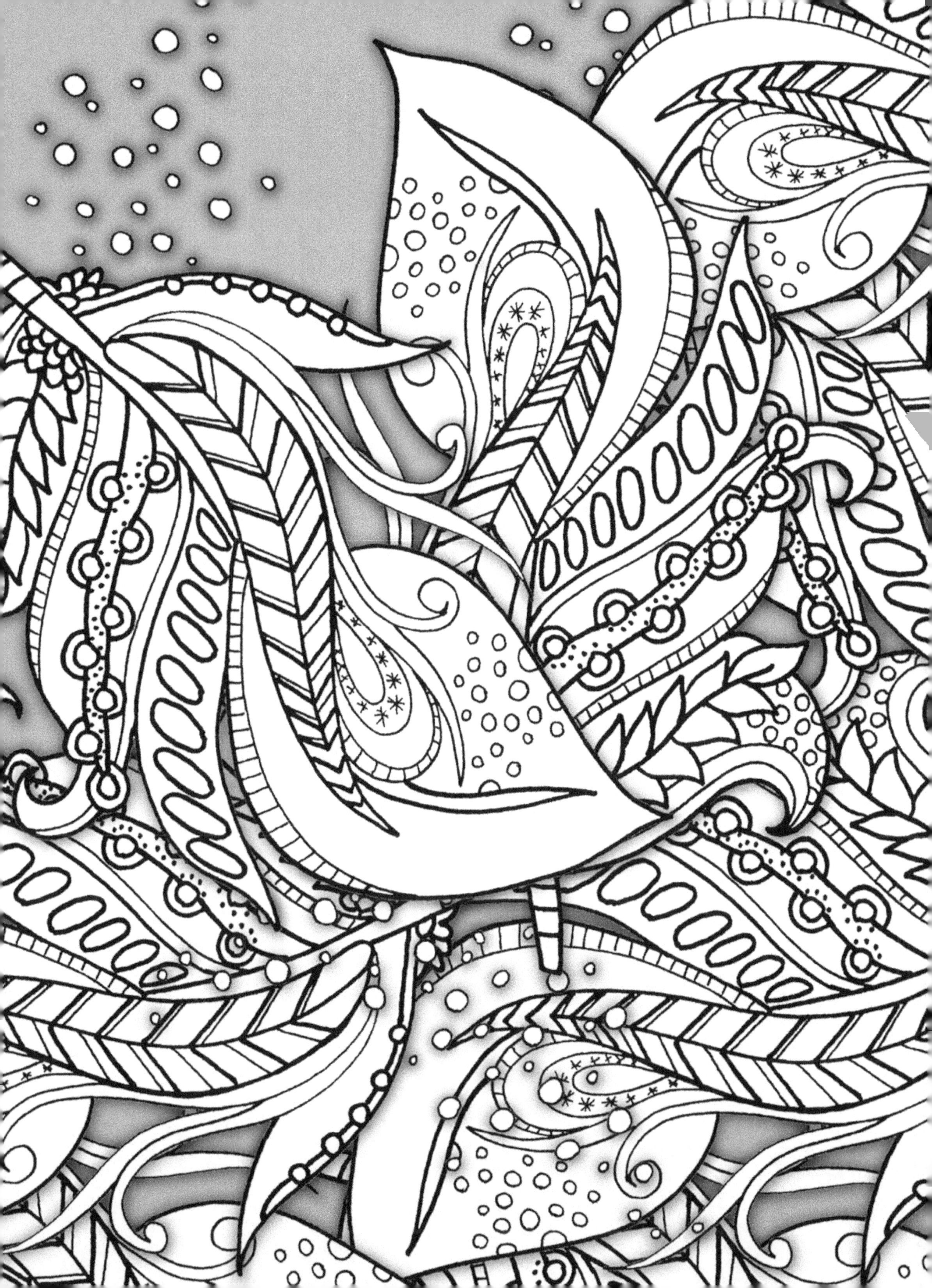

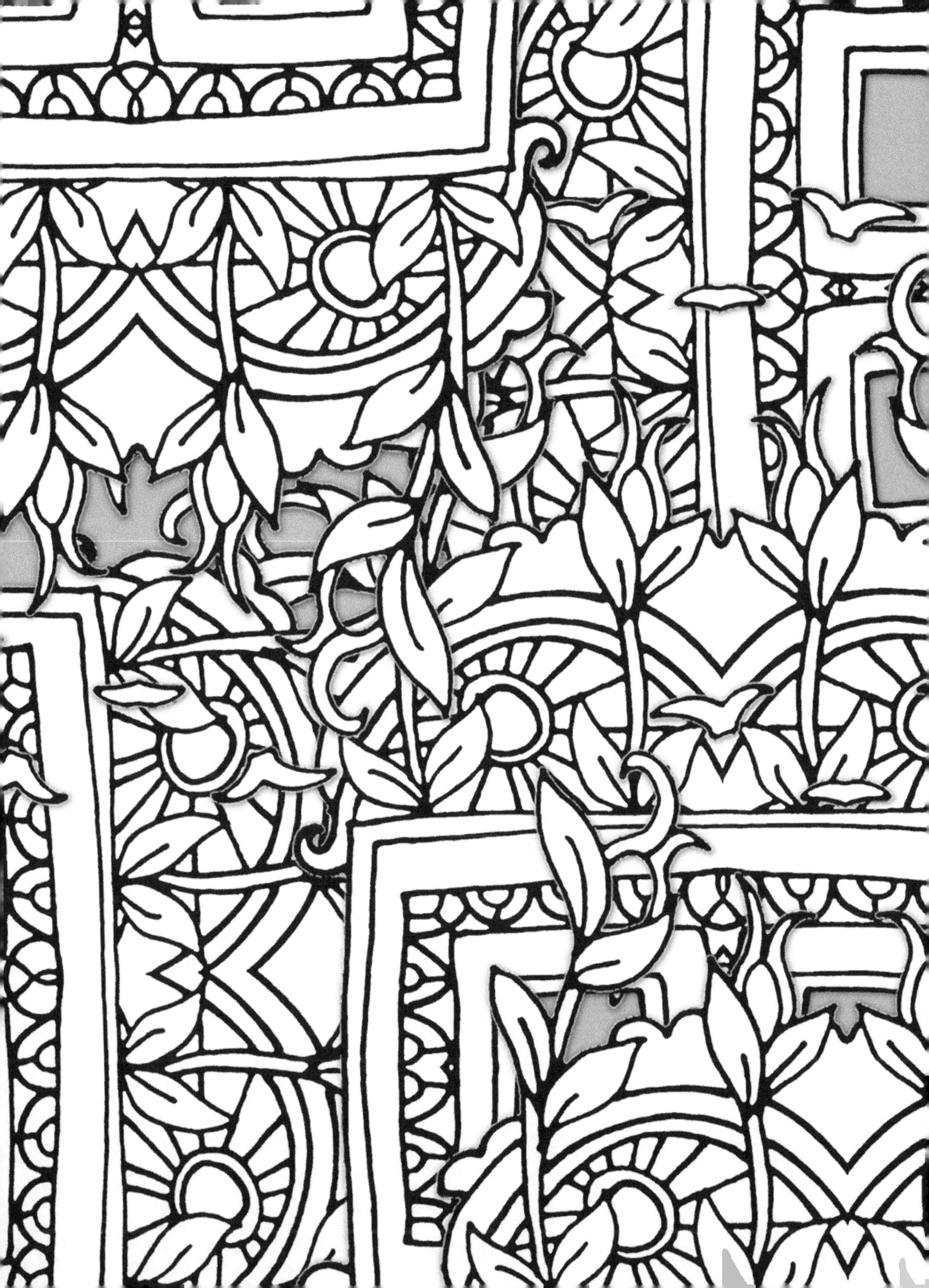

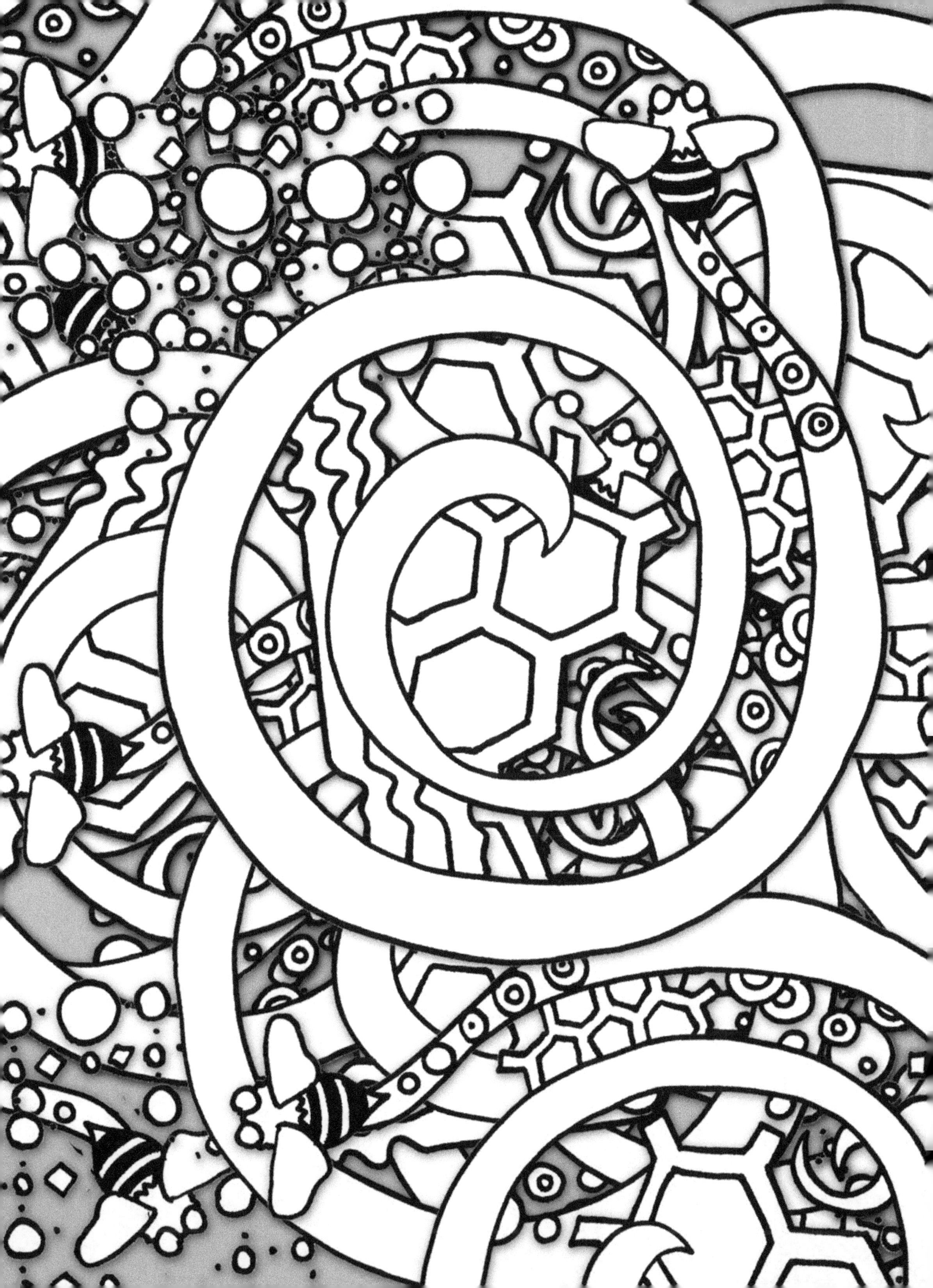

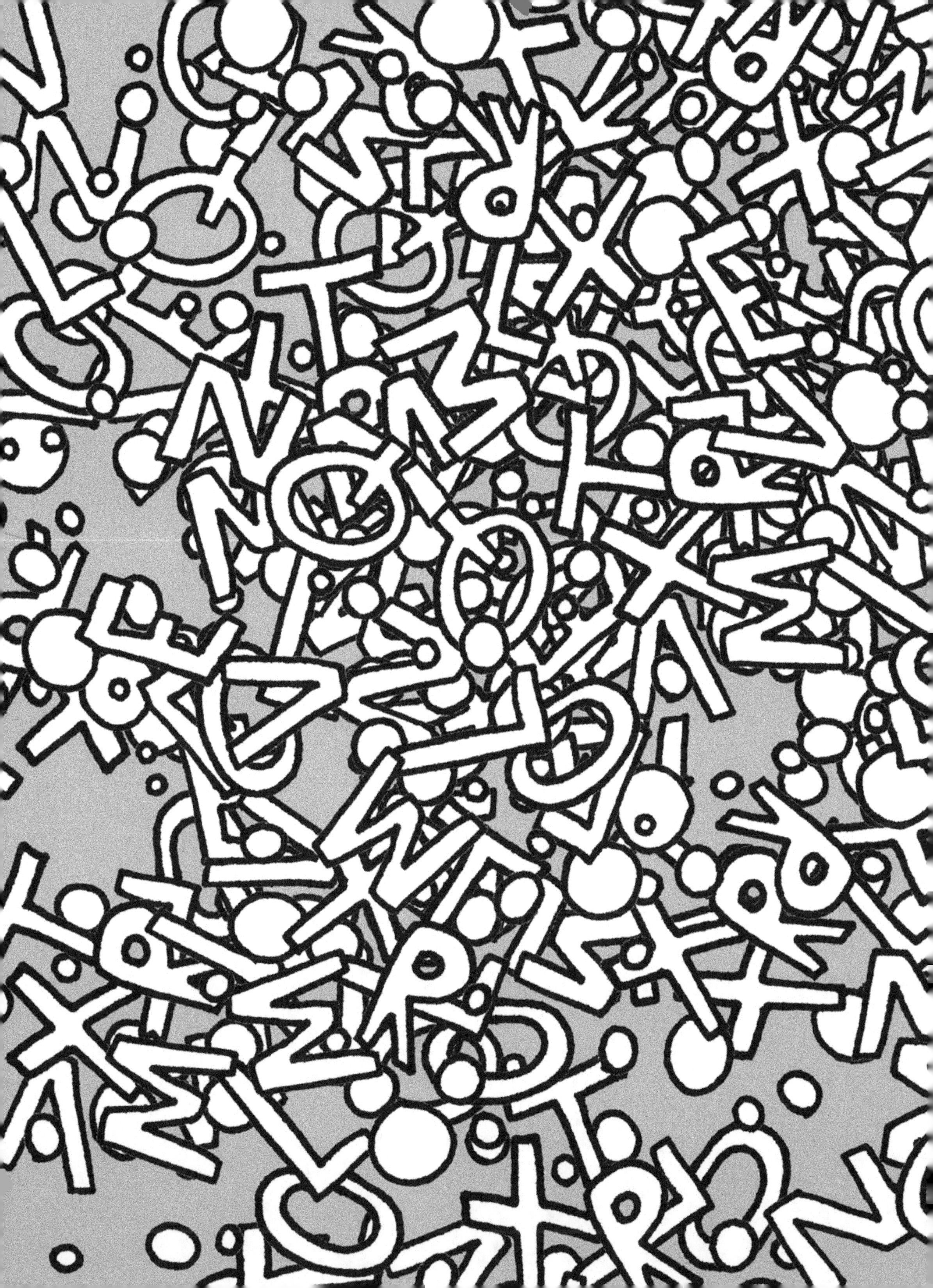

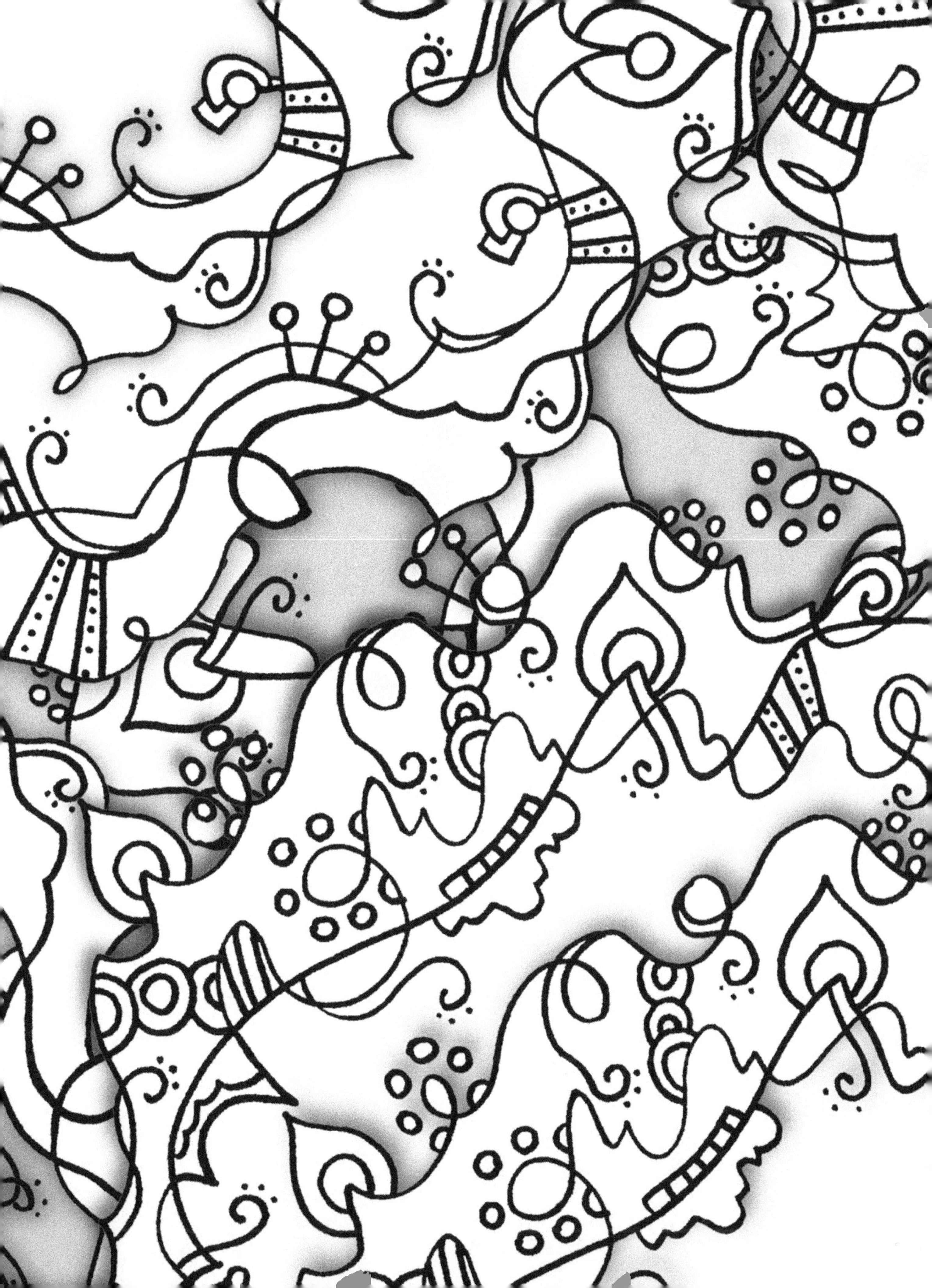

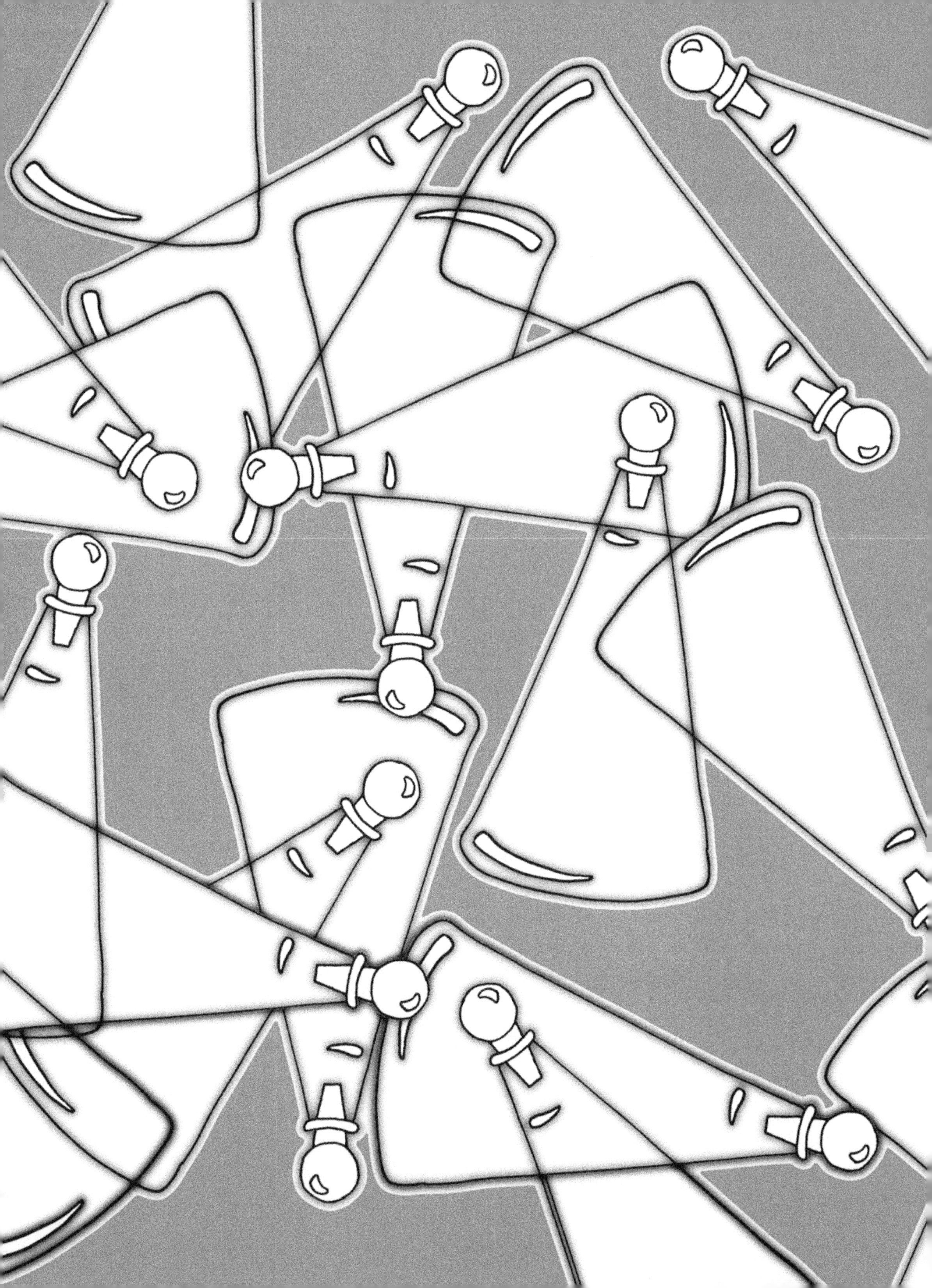

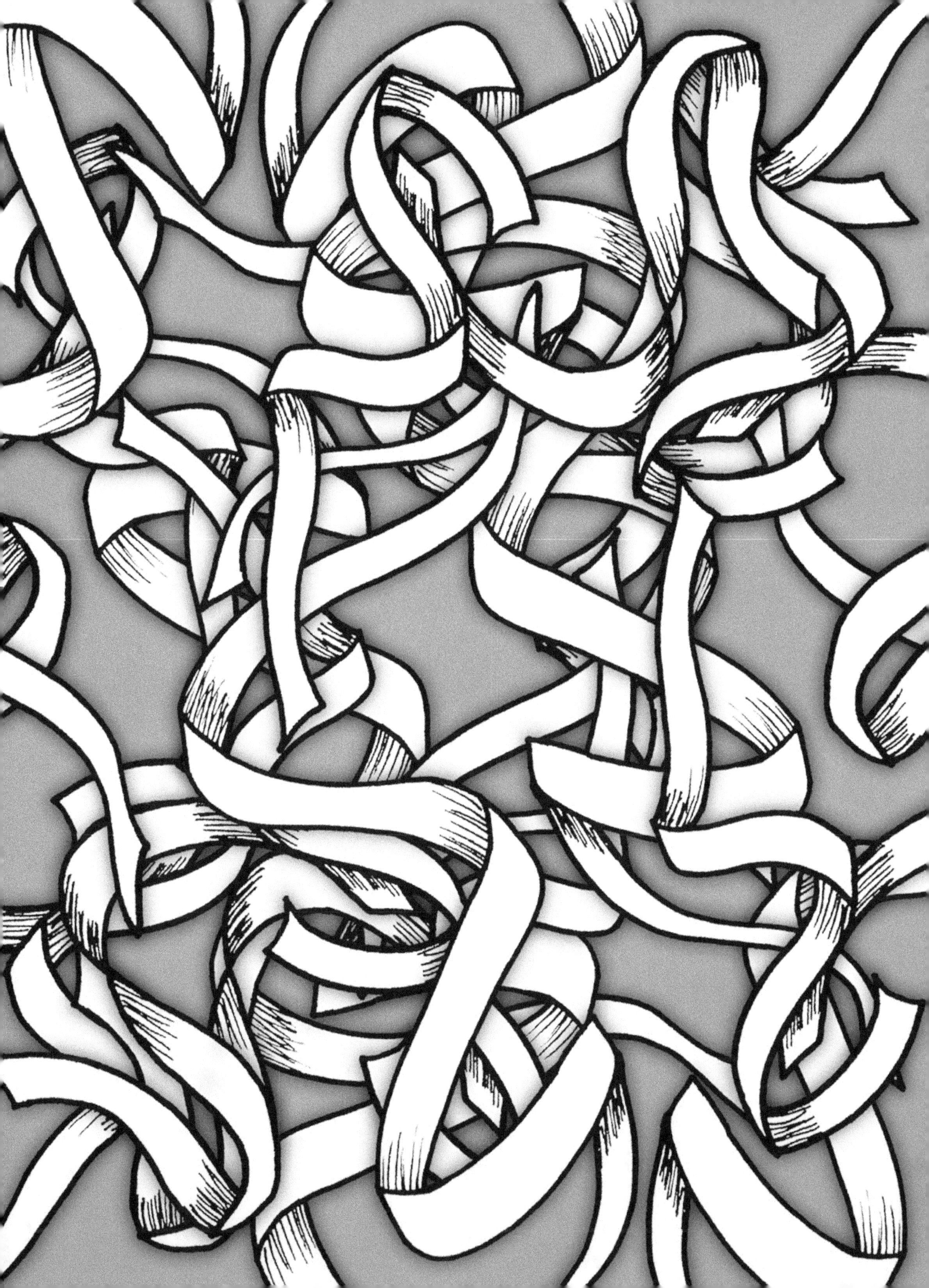

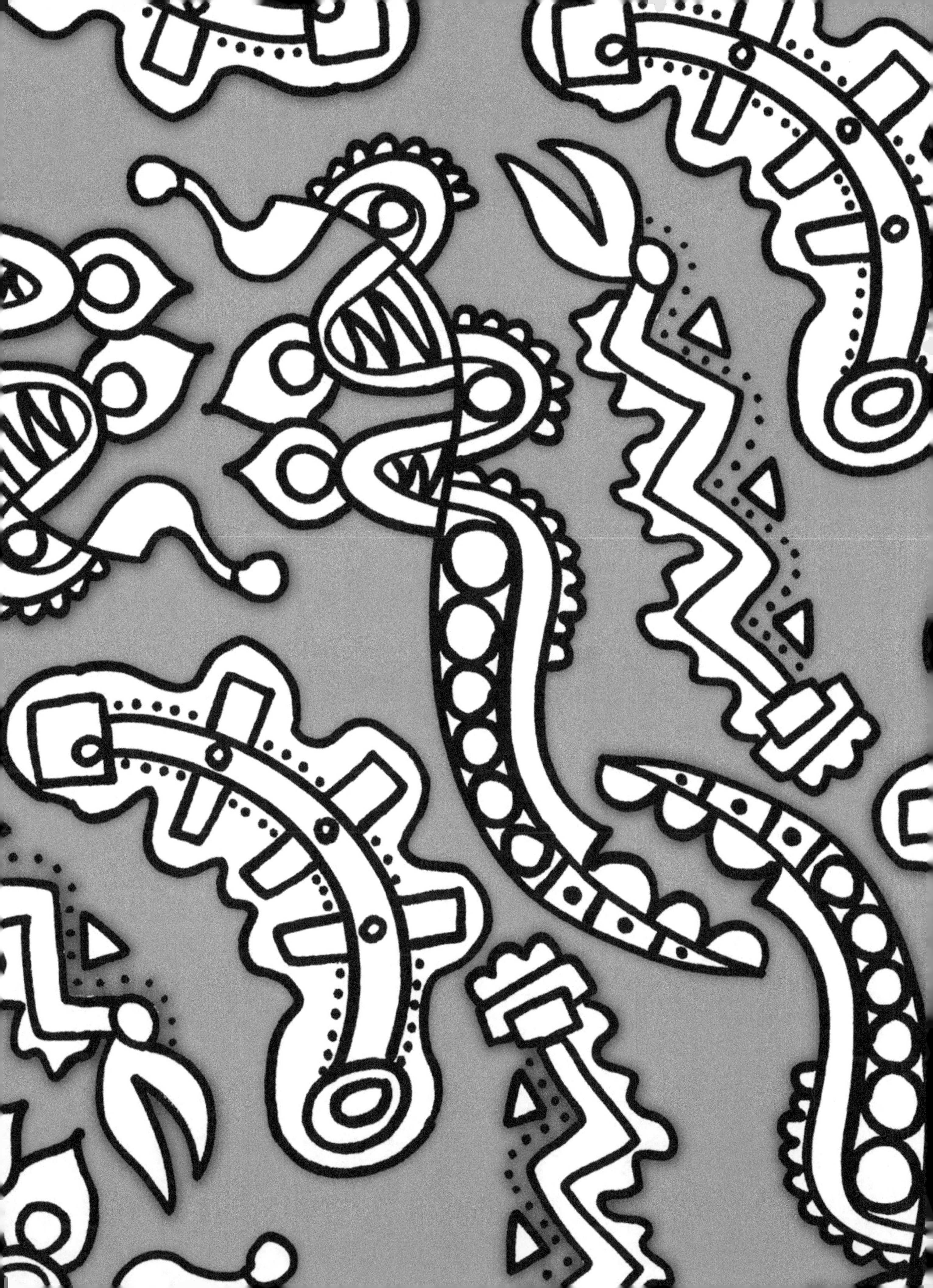

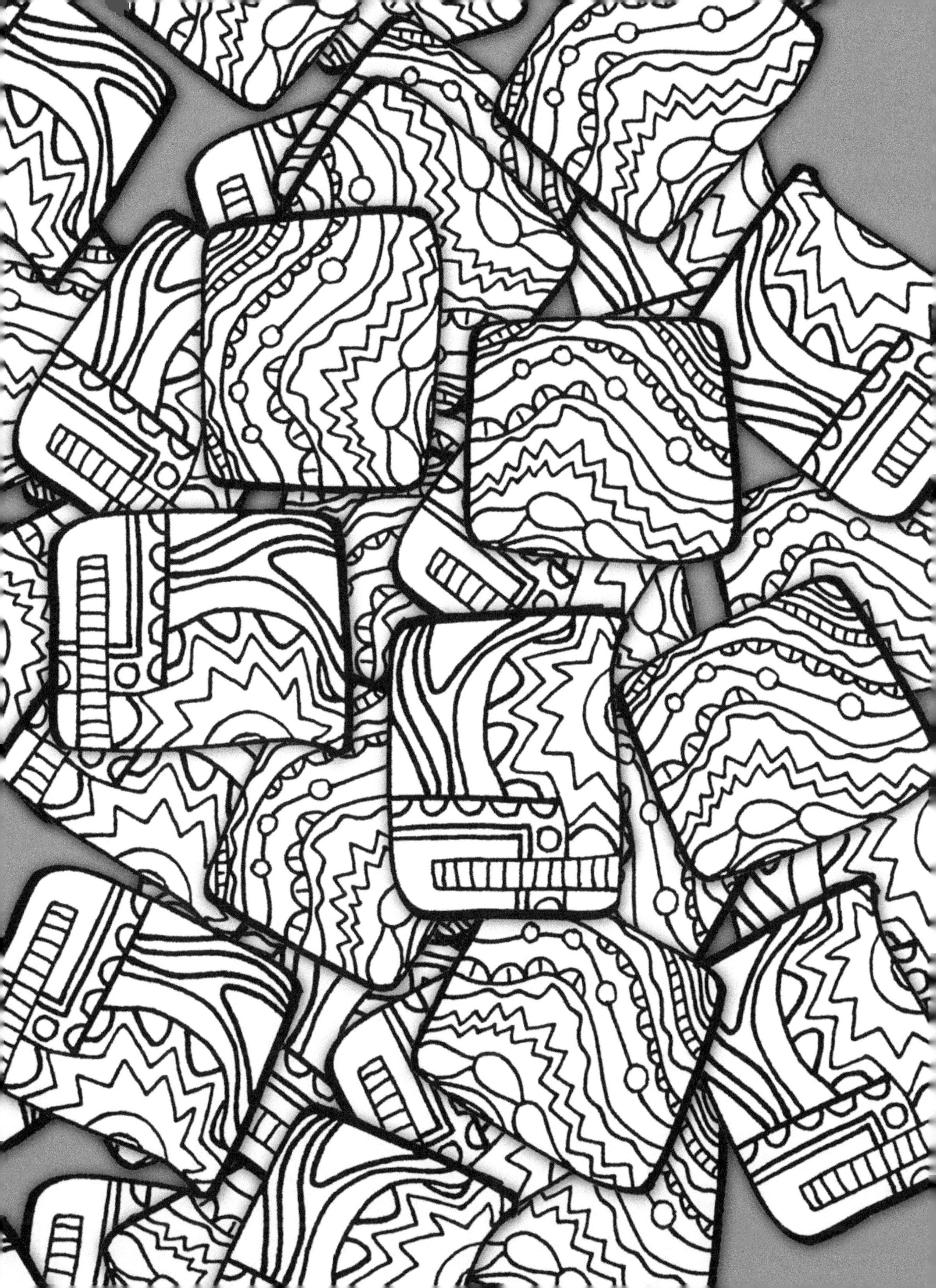

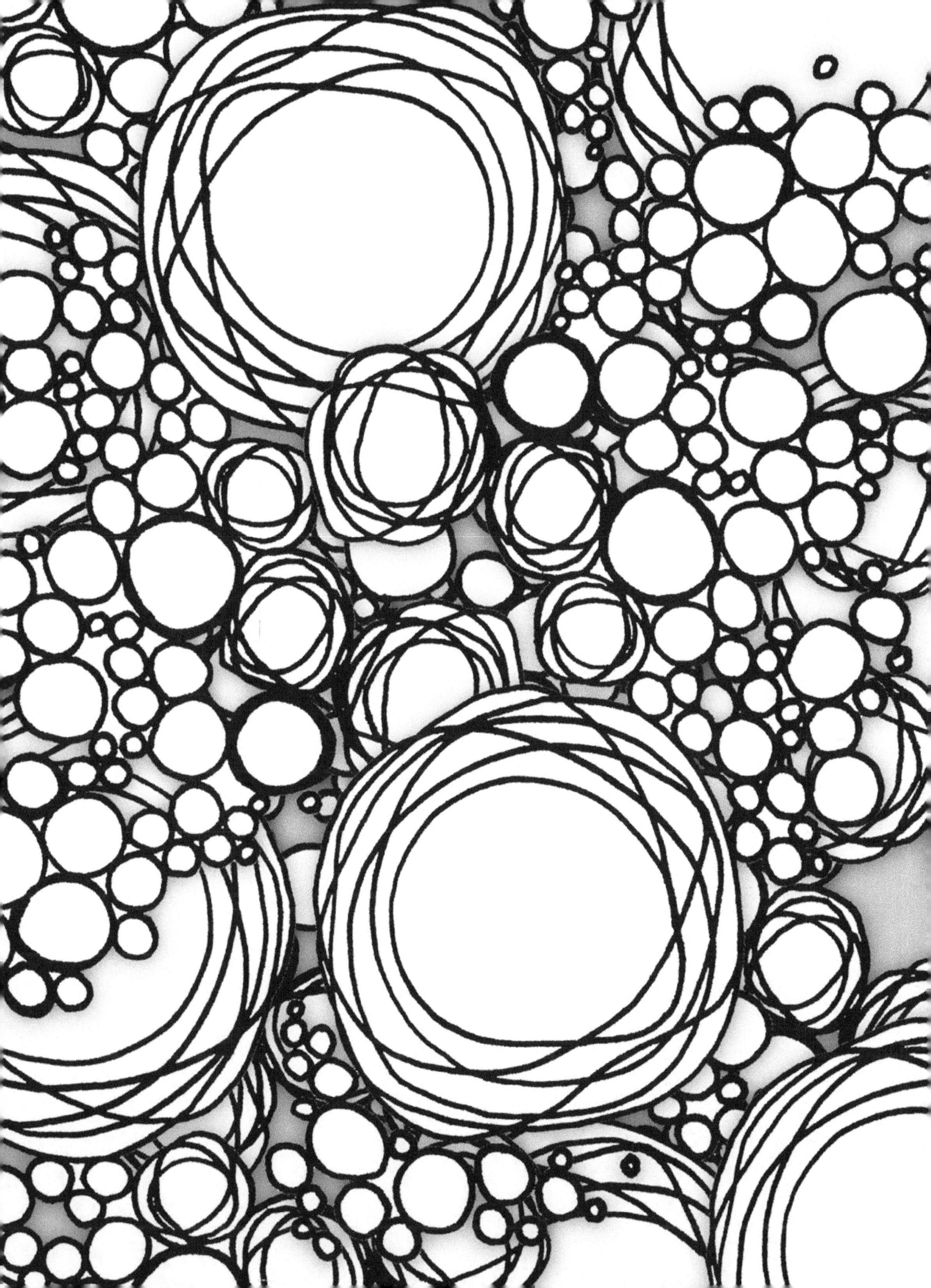

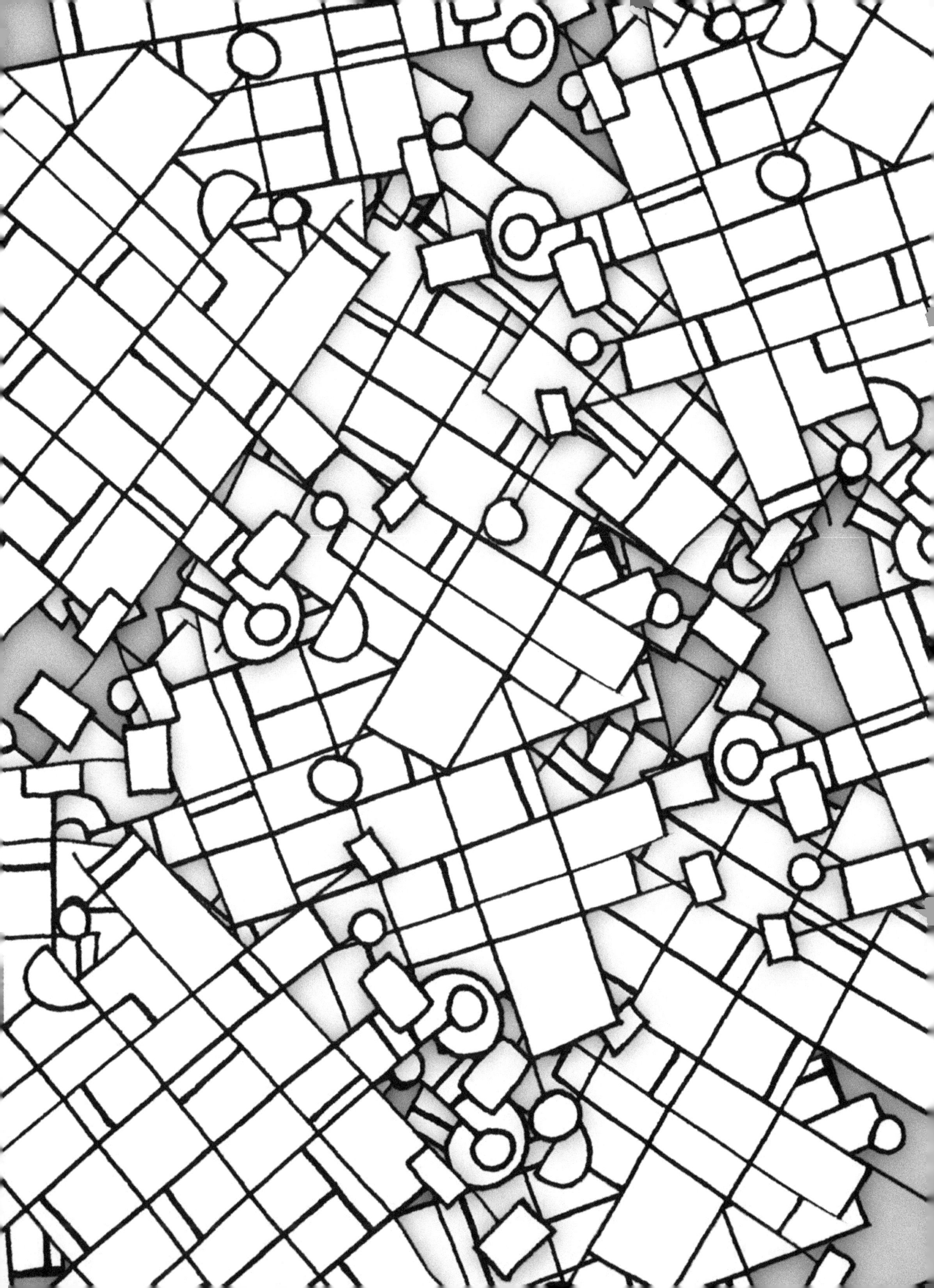

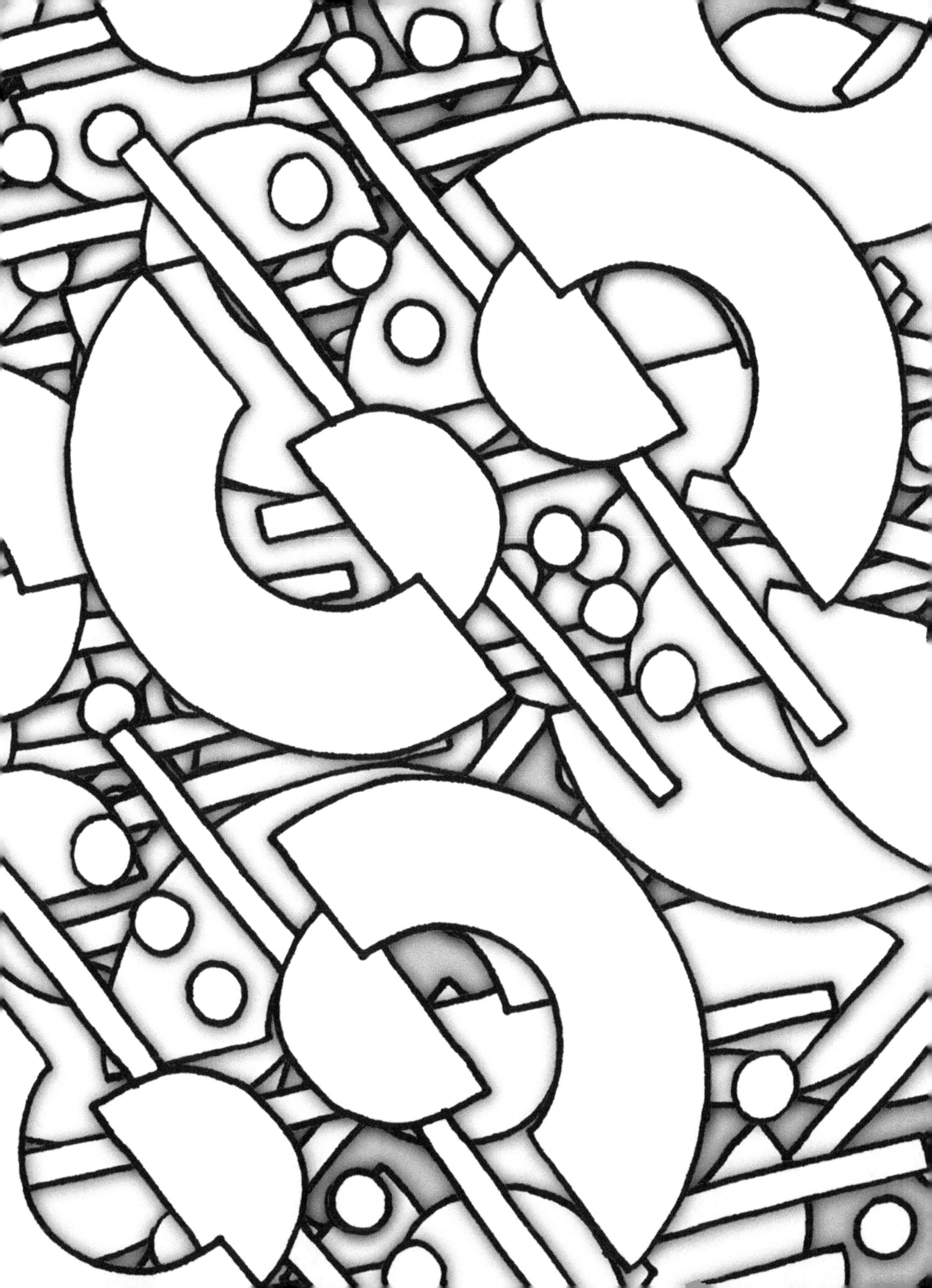

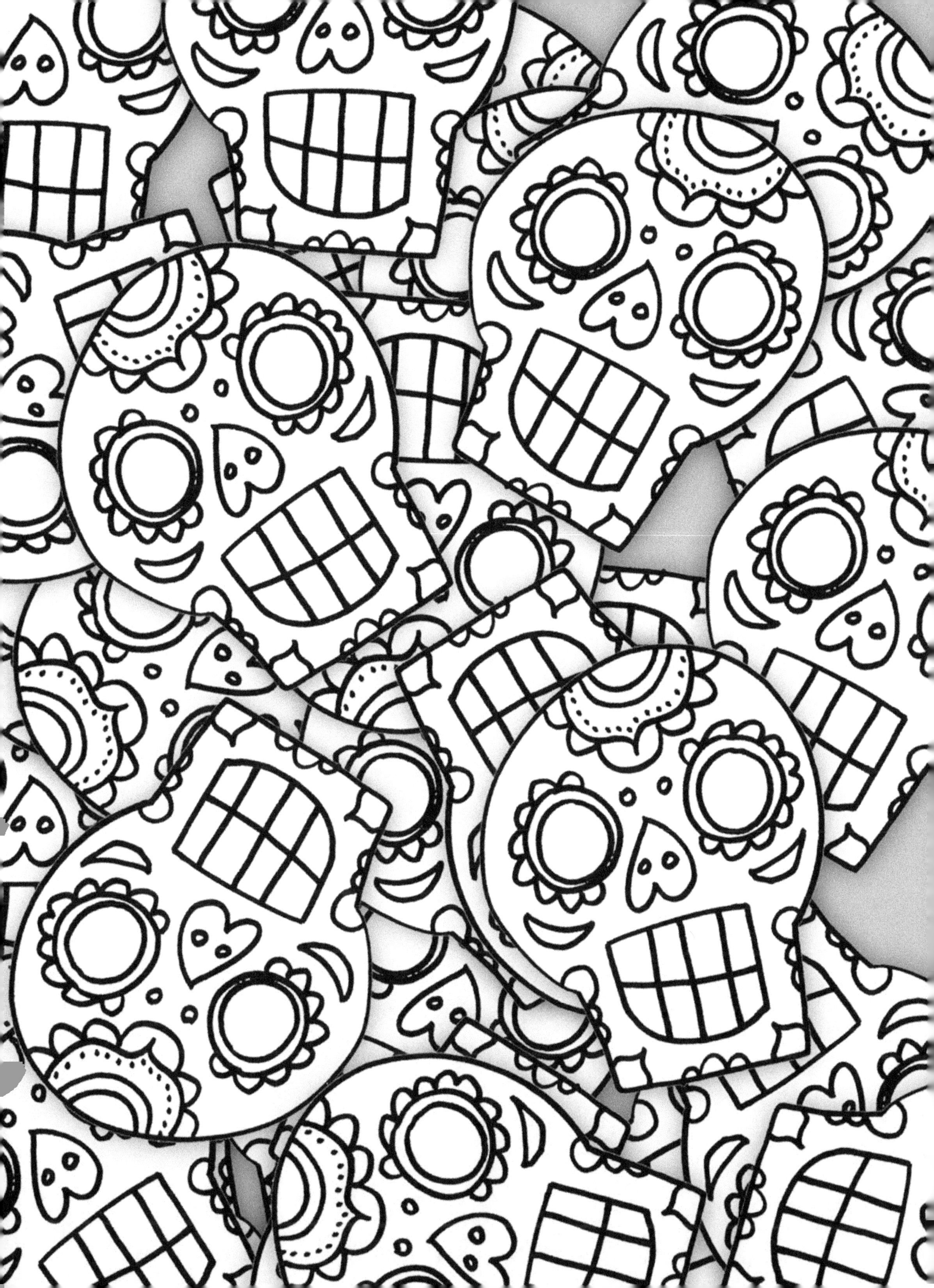

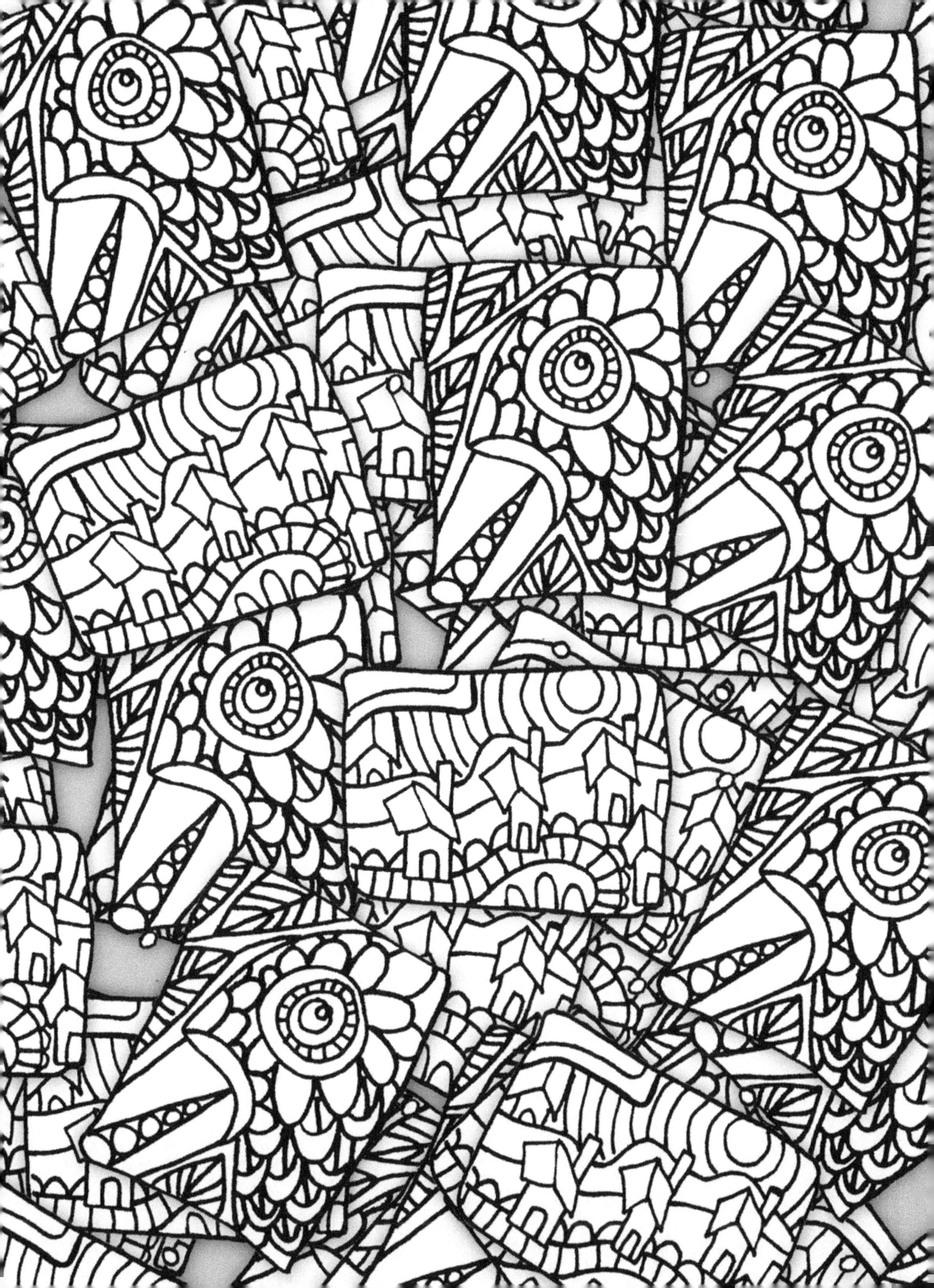

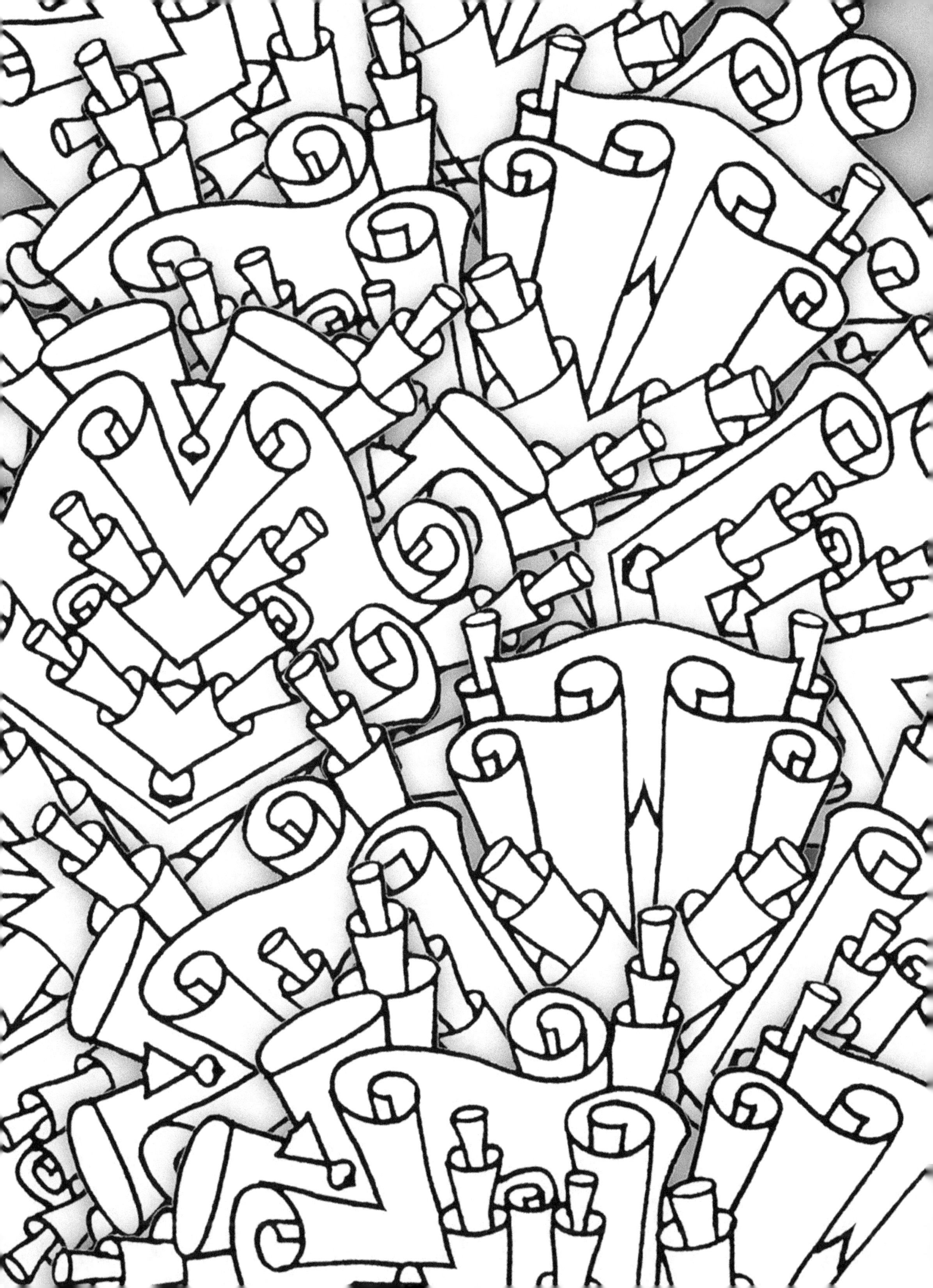

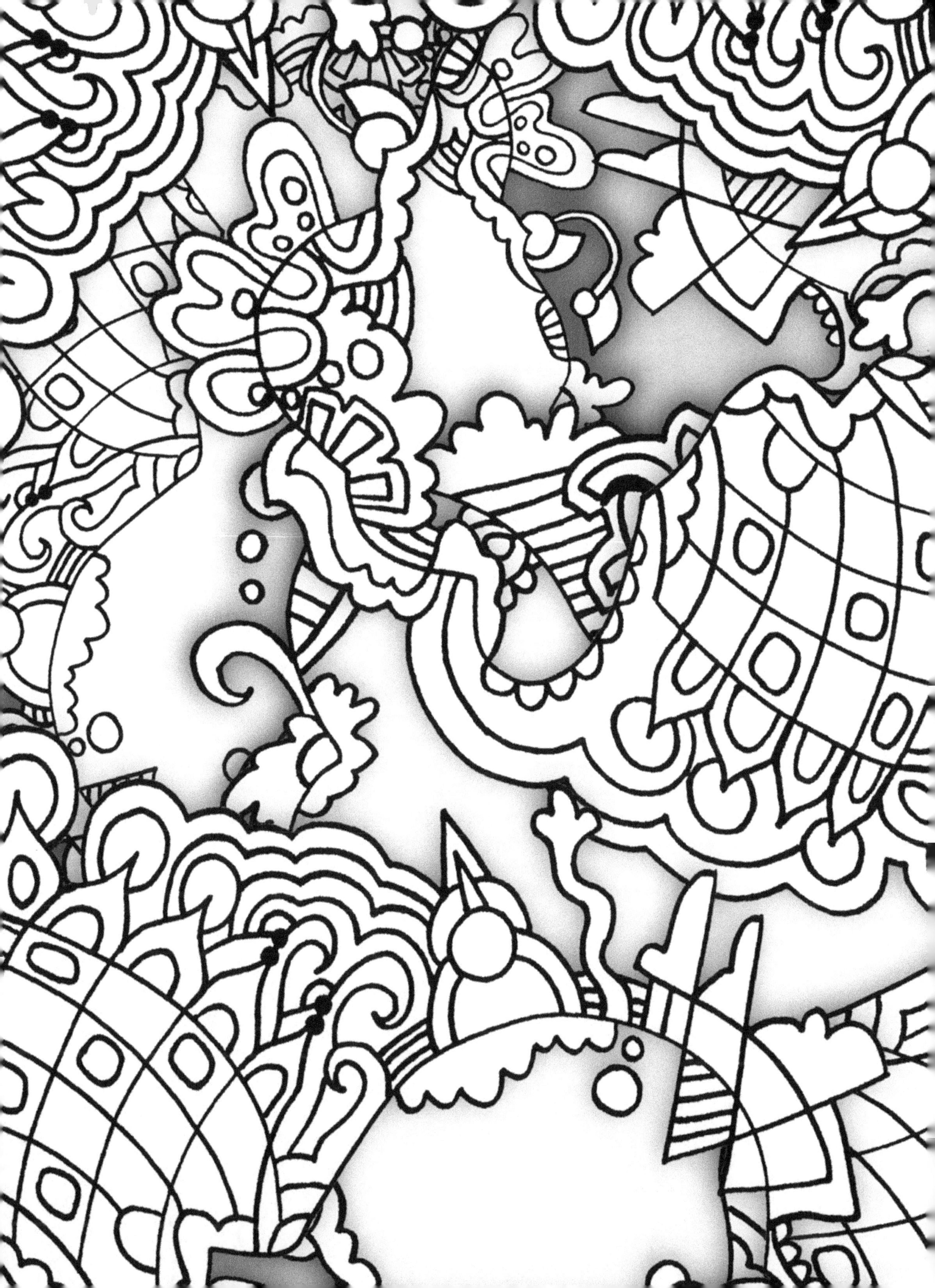

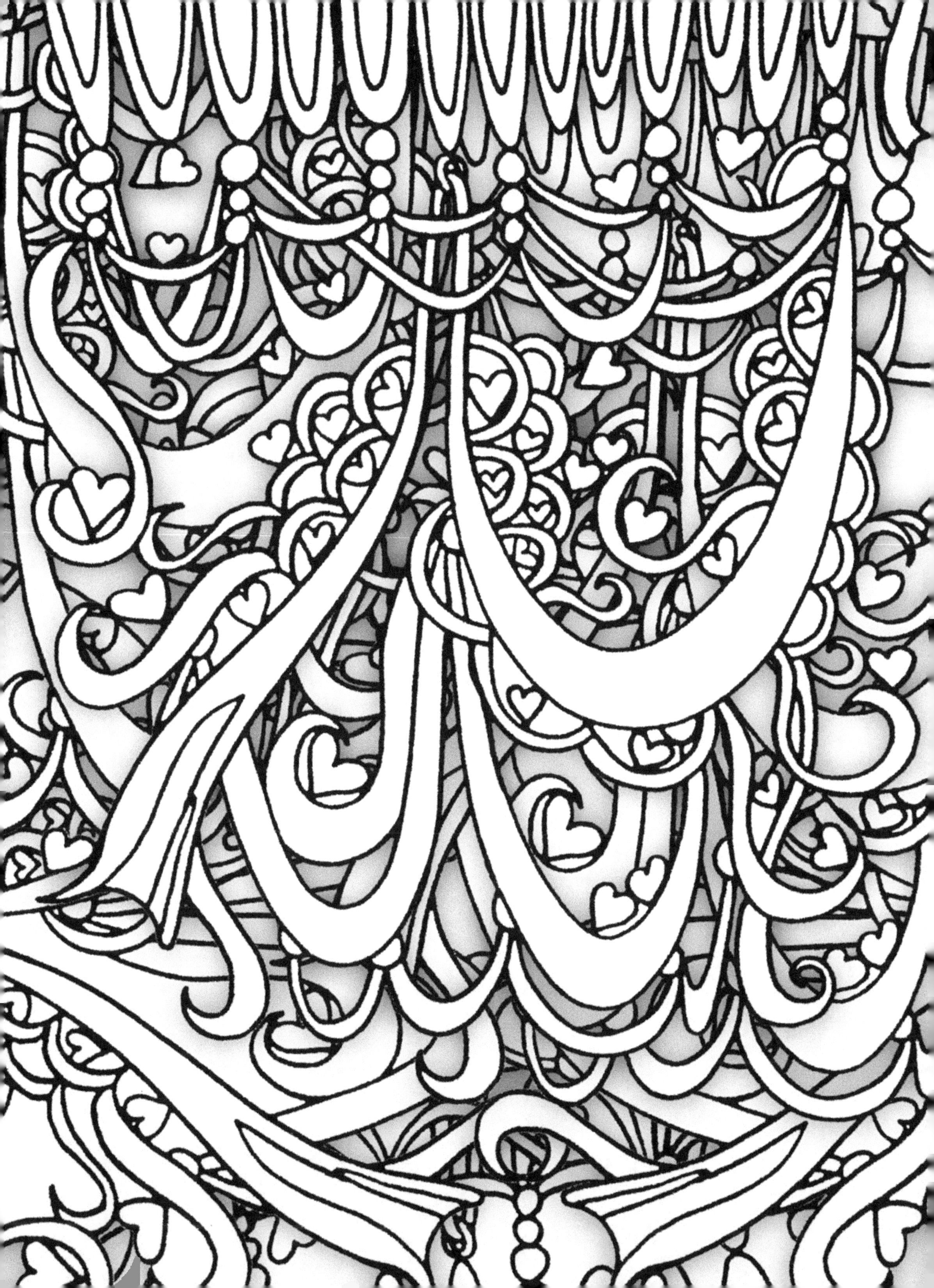

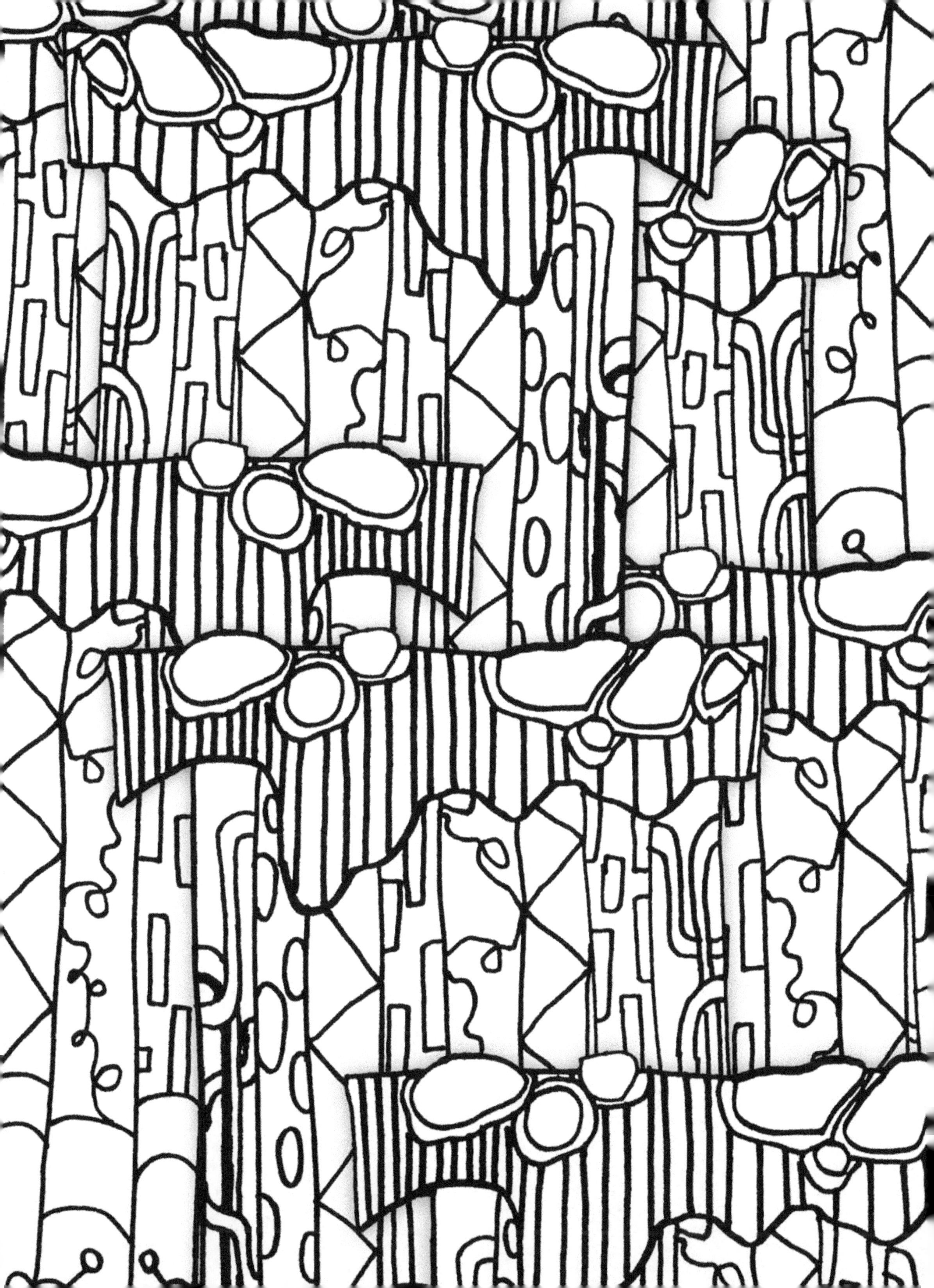

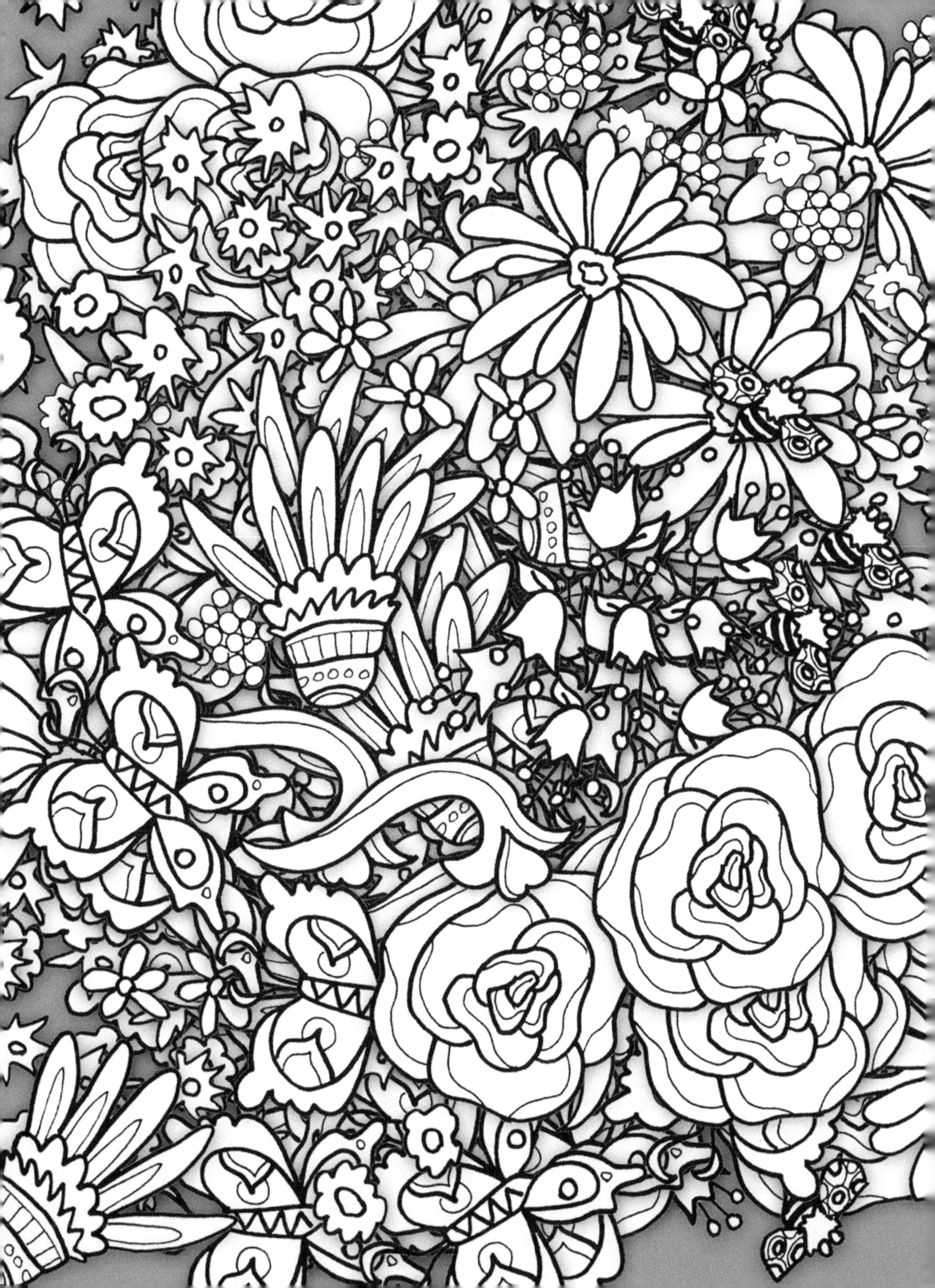

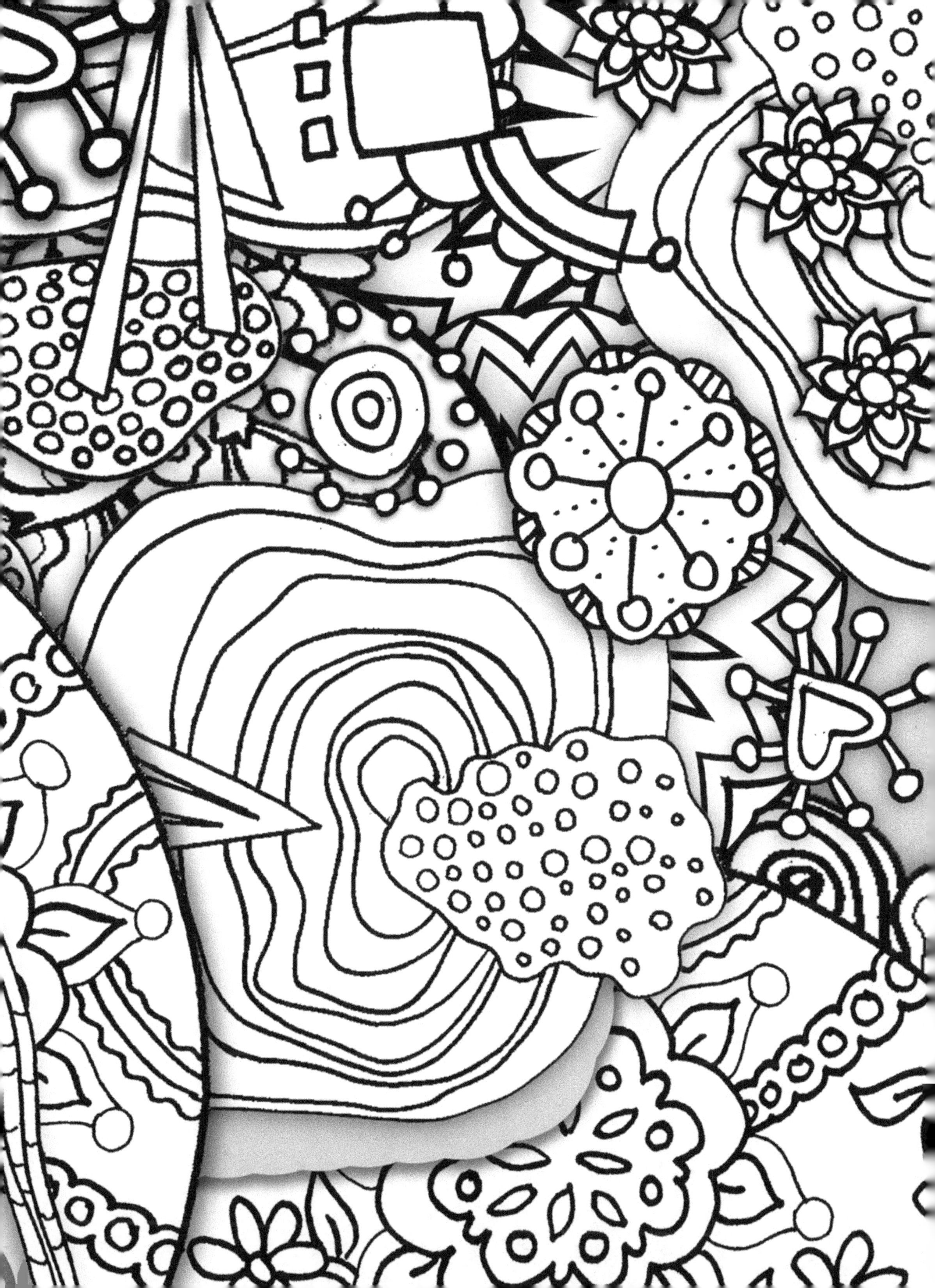

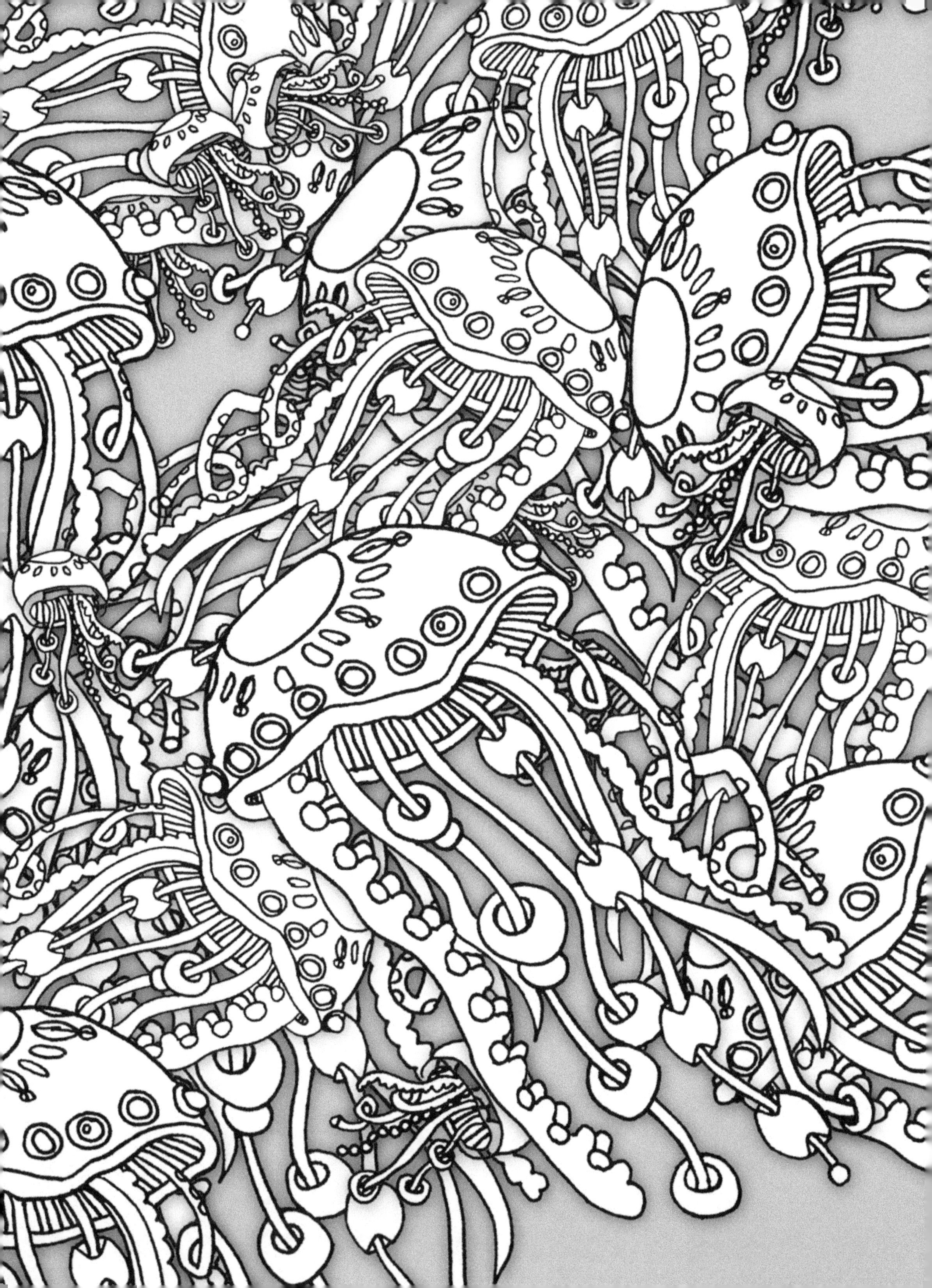

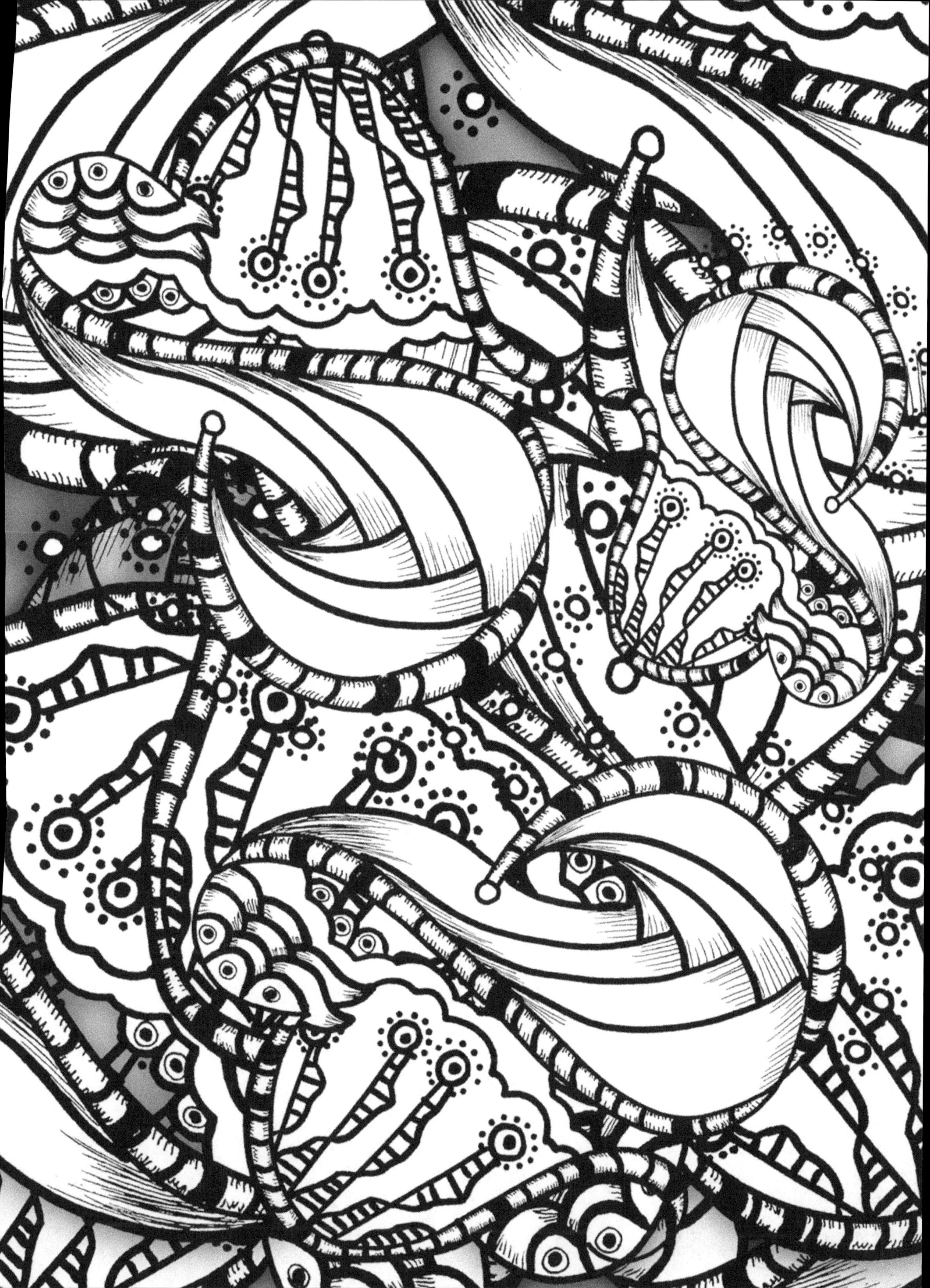

www.ingramcontent.com/pod-product-compliance
Lightning Source LLC
Chambersburg PA
CBHW080710190526
45169CB00006B/2316
9781523681716